THE
SCOT
WHO LIT THE
WORLD

THE STORY OF
WILLIAM MURDOCH
INVENTOR OF GAS LIGHTING

First edition

CONTENTS

For my father
James Stewart

Introduction

Scots are well known in the fields of science, technology and medicine and many are household names throughout the world. However lasting fame does not always go hand in hand with the significance of the contribution and can depend on successful self-promotion or on whose name was 'in vogue' at the time. A measure of luck is also necessary.

This book tells the story of one man who grew up in an Ayrshire village and took his skills to Birmingham, the heart of the Industrial Revolution of the 18th century. While the exploits of his contemporaries are well-documented, history has largely failed to recognise his unique contribution, even at times attributing his work to others. Although many vital papers have been lost, enough remains for us to learn a great deal about the debt society owes to his genius. Letters, reports, articles and books record not only events of his remarkable career but give insight into the life of a true human being who valued loyalty, integrity and creativity before profit and self-interest.

For every mile he walked to follow his dream, a year has passed with his name still only familiar in engineering circles and in places where he lived and worked. William Murdoch merits much wider recognition for his great many innovations and his brilliance which transformed the lives of millions. His greatest legacy was the invention of gas lighting.

Janet Thomson
June 2003

Although the first industrialised processes used water power, it was the introduction of the steam engine which really made the Industrial Revolution possible. Thomas Newcomen's crude "fire engine" developed in less than a century into the efficient, factory produced engines made by Boulton and Watt in Birmingham, sold all over Britain and exported abroad. A key figure in the manufacture of these improved engines was William Murdoch.

Starting as an engine erector for Boulton and Watt, he rose to become the mainstay of the firm as Engineer and Superintendent. Many of his inventions were ahead of their time, and had to wait for improved technology to make them practicable, but despite his fertile mind he remained a faithful servant to his friend and hero, James Watt. Several of the improvements attributed to Watt were due at least in part to William Murdoch, including the 'Sun and Planet' gear and the long-D slide valve. Murdoch's modesty has long overshadowed his undoubted mechanical genius; proper recognition of his life and work is long overdue.

Matthew J. Hume
Curator, Industrial History
North Lanarkshire Council Museums Service

Many reputations of engineering concerns were built upon the 'front man,' the man in direct contact with the customer who organised the labour, got all the materials on site at the right time and overcame any problems without the customer ever knowing they existed.

William Murdoch did all of those things in the infancy of mechanical engineering. He made the Boulton and Watt engines actually work and keep on working, although frequently faced with workmanship from Soho which was not of the best.

Any book which enhances the reputation of this practical, mechanical, engineering genius is to be warmly welcomed.

Geoff Hayes

1
Lugar

The story of William Murdoch (1754-1839) begins in mid-18th century lowland Scotland in the Ayrshire village of Lugar between Cumnock and Auchinleck. Only twenty miles from the birthplace of Robert Burns, Scotland's national bard, Lugar was set in rich agricultural land producing grain for the area's many corn mills. Situated just downstream of the junction of Glenmuir Water and Bellow Water is Bellow (or Bello) Mill whose name is thought to have come from the noise of water roaring through the pass to the mill dam.

Courtesy of The Kilmarnock Standard

Bellow Mill

Tenanted by the Murdoch family for over a hundred years, Bellow Mill became home to William's father, John, a miller *cum* wheelwright who moved there from nearby Bridgend Mill in Auchinleck around the time of William's birth. Eighteenth century millwrights were highly respected and well-known locally as men 'of superior attaintments and intellectual power.' Many successful technicians, engineers and inventors of the 18th and 19th century came from similar backgrounds. John's brother Robert was a local wright and joiner and another brother was miller downstream at Auchinleck Mill. Other members of this large and skilled family were John's two nephews who were master joiners and snuff box makers (Auchinleck, the first area to make invisible hinges, was famed for snuff box making). Later generations of Murdochs included clockmakers, master watchmakers[1] and engineers[2]

The Laird of Auchinleck Parish was Alexander Boswell who later became Lord Auchinleck. He was the father of James Boswell, famous companion and biographer of Dr. Samuel Johnson. In 1747 John Murdoch married Anna Bruce, sister of James Bruce (agent on the neighbouring Boswell Estate) who claimed descent from Robert the Bruce. They had seven children[3] of whom five survived beyond infancy.

---

1. Master watchmaker James Murdoch of Newton-on-Ayr (b. 1776) was the author's great-great-great grandfather.
2. Another Murdoch became senior partner in the Glasgow engineering business of Murdoch and Aitken, later renowned for locomotive and steam engine construction.
3. John and Anna Murdoch's children were: Jean born in 1748; Andrew in 1749 (who died in infancy); William 1754; Robert 1757; Mungo 1759; Euphemia 1762 (died in infancy) and James born in 1766.

Bellow Mill Cottage
c 1900

Beside Bellow Mill was a single-storey cottage that was home to William for almost 23 years. The house and surrounding land are now privately owned and the mill itself is still standing although largely in disrepair. Plans to build a museum nearby were abandoned in 1985.

Originally there were three pairs of millstones, two for shelling and finishing oatmeal but when the oatmeal plant was cleared out after a fire in the 1940's, a hammer mill for grinding proven-

Millstone
Bellow Mill

der (animal fodder) was built at right angles to the river bank. The mill dam was also rebuilt around this time to resist damage by ice when the river was in full flood during winter. After the water passes over the weir its name changes to become the River Lugar, flowing west as one of the many beautiful tributaries of the River Ayr which it joins at Barskimming Mill dam.

The young Murdochs spent many hours excavating a small cave from sandstone on the river bank just at the intake of the lade which conveyed water to the mill. Here William began experimenting with steam, boiling water in an old kettle over a fireplace. A long chimney made from tile pipe ran all the way up the banking and across the garden to connect with the cottage kitchen chimney. His attempts to produce light using gas from burning coal placed in a kettle are also believed to have originated here. It is said that William fixed a perforated thimble to the spout of the kettle and set the gas alight. If true, this would have anticipated the invention for which he is now famous by some twenty years. It is intriguing to imagine that some of his most significant inventions developed from boyhood observations in a dark and mossy cave.

In this most romantic of hideaways he was quite alone with his thoughts. Far away from the outside world he would hear nothing but the millwheel turning and the millstones grinding to the constant rush of the river flowing by and the singing of busy wagtails, blackbirds and the joyful song thrush.

Inside Murdoch's Cave

In common with all Ayrshire folk, the Murdoch family would have spent winter evenings around the kitchen fireplace which was heated by coal from local deep mines. This high quality cannel (candle) or splint coal (also known as parrot coal from the sound produced when burning) has a fascinating property. Jets of gas suddenly burst forth giving a bright flame, at times creating a soft, tarry mound on the coal's surface. It is very tempting for children to use a poker to work this tar back into the hole created by the jet, allowing another build-up of coal gas then sitting back to watch as gas once more rushes out, hissing and spitting flame.

A familiar sight in Ayrshire homes at this time was the earthenware container of burning cannel coal placed on top of the fire to give light as well as warmth to the room. Perhaps William and his friends recreated this scene in their cave. But it is in later years that William was to demonstrate the commercial significance of this phenomenon when he placed a large container of cannel coal on top of a furnace, collecting the gas to use as a substitute for oils and tallow in his greatest invention: gas lighting.

John Murdoch 1725-1806

William's father John Murdoch routinely walked to the village of Cumnock, a distance of two miles. Being a wheelwright, his familiarity with the wheel's properties and a natural flair for creative ingenuity led him to construct the first tricycle more than sixty years before Dumfriesshire blacksmith Kirkpatrick MacMillan produced his famous bicycle. Young William and his friends rode this remarkable wooden machine around the mill while its inventor could now make the journey to Cumnock in a much shorter time than by foot. Known locally as 'Murdoch's horse' that 'no mortal e'er could tire,' the cycle was propelled by lever handles attached to a ratchet on the axle. It was the object of much attention and talked about for a great many years. William later built on the design of the 'horse' when he began looking at ways to achieve locomotion using steam power.

John Murdoch was responsible for many innovations for Lord Auchinleck; he later designed a corn drying kiln and built a steam engine. He passed on many skills such as pattern-making to his son who accompanied him in much of his work. It appears that William had already learned enough stonemasonry from his father to be employed to build a bridge over the River Nith in Dumfriesshire, adding to his experience and giving him the opportunity to organise a workforce. A hundred years later, local stonemason John Murdoch erected a monument to commemorate William Murdoch. Interestingly, in the 16th century there lived a well-travelled Nithsdale mason, John Murdoch, who merited a tablet in the south transept of Melrose Abbey with the following inscription:

John Murdo sum tyme callit was I…
and had in kepying al mason work
of Sant Androys, ye hye kyrk
of Glasgu, Melros and Pasley
of Nyddes dayll and of Galway.

While William Murdoch's father was working on another invention, William himself became aware of the person who was to play a central role in his life and with whom he would develop a mutually rewarding working relationship as well as a true friendship. The engineer James Watt had formed a partnership with Dr. John Roebuck whose Carron Foundry in Falkirk (founded in 1760) made parts for the steam engine that would secure for Watt a prominent place in history.

Around 1766 John Murdoch designed and in- stalled the first cast-iron, toothed, bevelled millgearing at Bellow Mill, cast at the Carron foundry almost twenty years before Boulton & Watt installed gearing at Albion Mill in London. William, who by this time had been working with Boulton & Watt for seven years, worked on the new engine at Albion Mill and may well have been responsible for the large-scale application of his father's gearing. John Murdoch's original gearing was removed from Bellow Mill after his death in 1806 to take pride of place on the lawn of William's house in Birmingham. Millions of such cast iron gears were manufactured for use across the world making it one of the eighteenth century's major inventions.

Belonging to a family where invention was second nature, William's imagination would lead him to many elegant and practical solutions to problems which had challenged the best engineering minds of his day. He had already achieved a great deal while working with his father but, lured by the exciting new work being developed at the Soho Manufactory in Birmingham, he decided to take his skills to the heart of the new industry. He would leave Lugar to seek employment with Boulton & Watt.

Plaque at Bellow Mill
HS Tamley ARSA

The birthplace of William Murdoch
Inventor of lighting by gas
1754-1839
'That incomparable mechanic' Nasmyth
Erected by the North British Association of Gas Managers 1913

2
Historical Context

Mourn, hapless Caledonia, mourn, Thy banish'd peace, thy laurels torn!
Thy sons for valour long renown'd, Lie slaughter'd on their native ground:
Thy hospitable roofs no more Invite the stranger to the door;
In smoky ruins sunk they lie, The monuments of cruelty.

Tobias Smollett

As William Murdoch stepped out on his 250 mile journey to Birmingham in August 1777 he was about to enter a new age dominated by the very work he loved: engineering. A bold step indeed since the rural world he had known all his life was quite different to the industrial one which awaited him.

Until now his life had been in rural Ayrshire with people who shared his cultural and historical background. Over the next seven or eight days, his mind would no doubt have conjured up images of the great metropolis, the realities of which he could only guess. The journey itself would not have been an easy one owing to the poor condition of the roads at this time. But, undaunted, the adventurous youth made his way through mud and dirt tracks to reach his destination.

In the wider world, famous contemporaries of Murdoch's were busy shaping the future in their own field. Mozart, only two years younger, had already made his mark in Europe and seven-year-old Beethoven was set to join the ranks of great composers. Poet and artist William Blake was born three years after Murdoch while Goya and Gainsborough were already established masters of their art.

Lugar – Birmingham
250 miles

Scale: 50 miles

Map of Britain
showing distance walked
by William Murdoch
August, 1777

The Boston Tea Party had taken place only a few years earlier. This was two years after the American Revolution had begun and twelve years before George Washington became first president of the USA. France was about to join America against Britain and Captain James Cook was circumnavigating the world.

Politically, Scotland had recently undergone significant changes in which William Murdoch's ancestors played their part. His grandfather, John Murdoch, had been in the Royal Artillery at the beginning of the 18th century when Scotland had already gone through centuries of turmoil and transformation. The Union of Parliaments in 1707 (considered by many Scots as surrender to the English) and the succession to the throne of George I (son of Sophie the Electress of Hanover) led to the famous Jacobite endeavour to restore the Stuart dynasty in Scotland.

Bonnie Prince Charlie (Charles Edward Stuart) returned to Scotland in 1745 and proclaimed his father as King James III. Although met with enthusiasm in the Highlands, the Jacobite cause in Scotland was not widely supported and the lowlands proved to be staunchly Hanoverian.

William's father John Murdoch's military service is believed to have taken him to the Battle of Culloden as a gunner in Cumberland's army. This saw the end of the Jacobite cause with a loss of twelve hundred men in battle and almost two thousand more through execution, imprisonment and transportation. It was an episode of ethnic cleansing successful beyond the dreams of twentieth century dictators. Many thousands more Scots died in the infamous Highland clearances that destroyed civilisation in the north and saw huge swathes of land pass into conquering hands. This was the old world that John Murdoch inhabited.

Nowadays the phenomenal changes that took place in the twentieth century never cease to amaze older generations who lived through those times. No less fantastic must have been the social, industrial and technological advances witnessed by John during his eighty-one years. He was one of the first whose experience straddled both worlds. As the Industrial Revolution took root he adapted to changing conditions and set his son on the path to become one of the most important and original contributors to the new world.

3
Early Soho Years

BOSWELL: I do indeed come from Scotland, but I cannot help it …
JOHNSON: That, Sir, I find, is what a very great many of your
countrymen cannot help.

James Boswell: Life of Samuel Johnson

Matthew Bolton founded the Soho Manufactory off
Nineveh Road in Birmingham in 1772 and was joined
three years later by James Watt to begin the famous
partnership of Boulton & Watt, beacon of the Industrial
Revolution. Prior to setting up the partnership, Boulton
had discharged the debts of Watt's friend Dr. Roebuck
thus acquiring a two-thirds share of the steam engine
patent, the remaining one-third being retained by Watt
who brought his original experimental engine to Soho.
The legendary Watt engine with separate condenser
had its patent extended until 1800 and became the
mainstay of the Soho works.

As well as knowing of James Watt through his father's connection with Roebuck's Carron Foundry,
William would have been aware of the visit by James
Boswell to Soho in the previous year. Boswell probably
spoke to Boulton and Watt about the Murdochs' mechanical innovations at Auchinleck Estate and so
William could well have set out on his walk to Soho
with a certain anticipation that he would be, if not
favourably received, at least recognised on arrival.

The well-known account by biographer Samuel
Smiles of Murdoch arriving at the door of the Soho
works paints a picture of a young man twirling his hat

in his hands whilst being addressed by Boulton who asked what his hat was made of. The reply 'timmer, sir' (timber) prompted Boulton to enquire how it had been made to which Murdoch declared 'I made it mysel, sir, on a bit laithey of my contrivin'.' Suitably impressed since turning an oval shape on a lathe was as yet unknown and especially since he himself had even built the lathe, Boulton said he would enquire at the works and see if there was any position for the young mechanic.

However it is now thought that William was more likely to have travelled wearing more comfortable headgear such as a Tam O' Shanter and to have informed Boulton (in Watt's absence) of his skills as millwright and mechanic as well as his experience in pattern-making and casting. He possibly did show Boulton a wooden hat manufactured on his own self-made lathe by way of demonstrating his skills but he came to Birmingham equipped with a much more impressive range of experience and proficiency than this story suggests.

Whatever happened at their first meeting, Boulton was sufficiently impressed by the handsome young Murdoch to offer him work in the pattern shop for a wage of fifteen shillings (75p) a week, increasing this to 18 shillings when away from Soho. It was August, 1777 and William was only twenty-three years old. By the following year his reputation was established, Watt writing 'if William Murdoch is not at home he should be sent for immediately as he understands the patterns and care must be taken to avoid mistakes of which our engine shop has been too guilty.'

One job Murdoch was sent on was erecting an engine at Bedworth. So successful was his work that Boulton now judged him capable of going alone and so in March 1779 he was sent to his first solo job in Wanlockhead, the highest village in Scotland at 1500 feet and only twenty miles from his home. He took with him commendations from both employers, Watt introducing him as a very sober, ingenious young man with 'a good deal of experience under us in putting engines together (who) knows all the little niceties, the omission of which might cause a bad performance in your engine.' Used to pump water from the Mennockhass lead mine from a depth of 120 feet (36m), this was the second Watt steam engine erected in Scotland.

Hydraulic Beam Engine
Wanlockhead

4
Wanlockhead

Work at Wanlockhead had begun just after Murdoch left home to walk to Birmingham eighteen months earlier but local engineers had encountered problems with the new engine. On March 23rd Boulton wrote to the mine proprietor Gilbert Meason, 'We have this night dispatched William Murdock by the Sheffield coach with orders to proceed through Carlisle to Wanlockhead without delay ... He hath a good deal of experience in our engines and is capable of putting your people to rights in any matter they may not understand and we doubt not but he will acquit himself to your and to our satisfaction as he is a man we have a good opinion of. Pray don't keep him longer than necessary as we want him in Cornwall.'

Since communication had to be carried out by letter, records exist which show the nature of the work and the contributions made by the men involved. In early May, Watt wrote to Murdoch saying he had received his letter of April 29th giving details of problems with pipe joints when the engine was under steam. Watt gave Murdoch directions on how to overcome these problems largely due to softening of putty in the joints. One solution was to wrap rope yarn around the neck of each screw and then tighten the screws one by one when the engine was warm. Another involved using thin putty and waiting until it had hardened with the heat before increasing the steam pressure. Watt also wished to know how much coal would be needed to power the engine.

He suggested that Murdoch kept a note of any proposals he made to the local engineers so that in the event of a dispute it could be seen whether they had followed his advice. Towards the end of May, Watt wrote to Meason 'I am extremely happy to hear that your engine has set out so well. May it prosper and discover much riches.' However a few days later the engine suffered some kind of accident while being operated by Wanlockhead's famous engineer, George Symington. Watt supposed this to be the result of an over confidence but wrote that Symington showed 'a great deal of ingenuity and abilities in what he has done, and in adhering to the directions I formerly sent he was not to blame, but he ought to have considered that Murdock had an opportunity of knowing my mind, of a later date than the directions and certainly would not be foolish enough to controvert my orders without reason.'

On July 29th Murdoch wrote to Watt expressing surprise at Meason's report to Watt on the question of how much coal the engine required before any had been weighed for that purpose. Murdoch described in great detail two trials made in the presence of Symington and others. He wrote 'I have made many experiments on the engine and find that when it goes six strokes per minute it requires ten hundredweight of coal in the 24 hours.' This was less than half the amount of 2,500 lbs reported by Meason.

The following week Watt asked Meason to give the young man money for his return journey south and sent his final instructions to Murdoch regarding the engine stroke. William would appear to have expressed a wish to return by an alternative route but Watt was quite specific, writing 'you will get money from Mr Meason or the agents at the mine to pay your charges home and come directly for Birmingham as you are wanted and there is (no) occasion for your going to Newcastle which is 60 miles out of your road.'

Only later did Watt discover that Murdoch had rearranged the working-gear at Wanlockhead to allow steam from the exhaust shaft to work the steam valve, improving the engine's performance. Despite Watt's great reluctance to allow anyone to tamper with his design (still under patent), he had to admire Murdoch's ingenuity which would lead to many hundreds of innovations over the years. When another Boulton & Watt employee, Jabez Hornblower (brother of Jonathan), sought permission to adopt Murdoch's Wanlockhead modification on the engine he was working on, Watt refused but shortly afterwards sent Murdoch to replace Hornblower. This underlines the confidence and trust Watt had in Murdoch.

It was soon clear that Murdoch's decision to take his talents to Birmingham was a good one. Within the company he was given opportunities that he would never have had at home in Ayrshire. He was to share a stage with the cream of Britain's engineering and, despite setbacks that could have discouraged a weaker man, he successfully forged a fifty-year association with Boulton and Watt.

5
Boulton & Watt

To appreciate the good judgement of young Murdoch in seeking out Watt and Boulton it is necessary to look more closely at the partners themselves and what made them who they were.

Matthew Boulton

Matthew Boulton (1728-1807) was the son of a Birmingham business-man whose firm pro-duced buckles, buttons, snuff boxes and trinkets. At the age of 17 he joined his father's business and

Statue of Matthew Boulton
W Bloye

was married four years later. But his wife died and he married her sister who bore him two children. By this time Matthew Boulton was in charge of the company and was able to devote time to the pursuit of scientific knowledge, his abiding passion.

In 1726 the business moved to new premises near the Handsworth area of Birmingham, and became known as the Soho Manufactory. The name is thought to describe the sound of the hunting horn depicted on a local inn-sign. As Boulton developed a select range of products from silver plate and sterling silver to ornate candelabras and clocks, Soho's fame spread throughout fashionable society in Britain and Europe.

The Boulton family lived in the impressive Soho House set amidst landscaped gardens and picturesque parkland (now a museum). Matthew Boulton was a consummate businessman who welcomed many visitors to Soho and took responsibility for the welfare of his employees. His considerable scientific aptitude combined with his natural gift for socialising earned him membership of Birmingham's elite Lunar Society which often met at his Soho home.

Under Boulton's control, the Soho Manufactory was perfectly placed to play a central role in an increasingly industrial and commercial society. He was aware of the potential of steam power and when he learned of the work of James Watt he persuaded the Scotsman to join his business, beginning a thirty-year partnership that became famous throughout the world.

James Watt

James Watt (1736-1819) was born in Greenock, the son of a merchant and shipwright and grandson of a mathematician. His gift for invention was encouraged by his father and the young Watt's reputation as a budding mechanic was soon established. The

Statue of James Watt
W Bloye

only surviving child in the family he had the misfortune to suffer ill health from an early age. Throughout his life he was plagued by illness and had an intense concern for the health of others as well as his own.

29

His father's fortunes were to decline before James reached the age to begin university, but although this deprived him of the opportunity for formal study, he was introduced into Glasgow academic circles through his mother's family. Watt's nature was such that he deplored the emerging cultural liberalism and sided with the Presbyterian clergy who denounced artistic expression as the work of the Devil. For him the pleasures of intellectual pursuits were sufficient. But circumstances dictated that he earn a living and so he set his sights on becoming a mathematical instrument maker which took him to London where he completed the four year training course in only a year.

On his return to Glasgow he gained considerable knowledge and experience through contact with some of the best teachers and scientists in the city. He married his cousin at the age of 28 only to suffer great heartbreak when she died nine years later. After her death he was unable to form a close attachment to anyone else. When he remarried he chose his new partner for her efficiency as a housewife and avoided becoming emotionally dependent on others for fear of losing them.

Watt's interest in the field of steam engine design grew from contact with scientists he met in Glasgow. By this time steam technology had already undergone many important developments with associated protection of ideas by improvement in patent laws. With Watt's invention of the separate condenser, the steam engine overcame earlier limitations in the larger Newcomen engines which first appeared around 1712.

<u>*B&W*</u>

Boulton's shrewd business eye recognised the value of Watt's genius and Watt saw opportunities both in engineering and socially by aligning himself with Boulton. Having secured a twenty-five year patent on Watt's engine through his persuasive representation to a Parliamentary Committee, Boulton succeeded in finalising arrangements with Watt to join him in Soho.

This was a time of political unrest and the years leading to the French Revolution saw an increase in demand for industrial and military hardware. Travel became easier with the construction of new roads and the movement of cargo and fuel was facilitated by the growing network of canals. All of this was good news for the new partnership since the market place was wide open and hungry for their products.

The way ahead was not always a smooth one though. The relationship between Boulton and Watt, although highly successful and based on mutual admiration, was not always free of frustration. Watt was a man who remained convinced of the superiority of his own inventions therefore uncomfortable at the thought of adopting the ideas of others. Boulton usually knew a good thing when he saw one and so it was not uncommon for a difference of opinion to arise between the partners. The possibility that other engineers would develop ideas not protected by patent put further pressure on them when agreement on a new design could not be reached. When it appeared that someone else had patented his ideas, Watt reacted with characteristic vehemence that often left him ill with migraines and unable to function. One disagreement arose around 1780 in the early days of the rotary engine. Boulton firmly believed in the future of rotary motion whereas Watt, who nevertheless went on to patent five versions of his steam wheel, showed no such enthusiasm, concluding that little profit lay in pursuing this idea.

Watt's energies remained firmly bound up in his steam engine which he rightly saw as a vital part of the business. Boulton however judged that the time would come when the company would need another direction and held to his faith in the rotary engine.

BMW

This gives an idea of the scene in which Murdoch was to play his part. The partnership of Boulton and Watt was undoubtedly successful. Both men were motivated not only by scientific endeavour but by profit and in an increasingly capitalist society their methods were handsomely rewarded.

Murdoch, a man of equal genius, was an invaluable asset to the company. Boulton and Watt were to derive incalculable benefits from his contribution to the firm. He went on to invent most of their machine tools and to give unparalleled service. They could have broadened their horizon and taken him on board in an equal capacity with consequences that can now only be dreamed of. Instead they chose to maintain the status quo with Boulton advancing the fortunes of his protégé

Watt who adhered firmly to his own ideas above all others. Nevertheless Murdoch's talents flourished, perhaps because he cared so little for profit but revelled in the environment which had brought brought him all the way from home and now gave him the scope he needed to exercise his skills.

Statue of William Murdoch, James Watt & Matthew Boulton

W Bloye

Murdoch's simple and efficient steam wheel design would overcome many of the problems Watt had been unable to solve and for over thirty years his device powered Soho's workshop tools. He broke the deadlock over rotary motion by inventing the beautifully conceived Sun and Planet gear. Together with Watt's double action and parallel motion this allowed the company to develop rotative power. Long before this it had already become obvious that his was no ordinary talent. So convinced were Boulton and Watt of young Murdoch's value, they decided to send him to manage the company's crucial and demanding Cornwall enterprise.

6
Cornwall

William Murdoch arrived in Cornwall to manage Boulton & Watt's interests in late autumn or winter of 1779, only two years after his career with them began. He was to form a very special bond with Cornwall, making it his home and becoming accepted by the Cornishmen as one of their own. But such were the conditions in which he found himself he literally had to fight his way into the affections of the people. This was a time of fierce competition from outside Cornwall, threatening the prosperity of the mines and the livelihood of the miners. The mine owners fought hard to maintain the price of copper and resist attempts by rivals to force cuts in production. With Boulton's help they created a cartel, buying the entire output and selling it at a fixed price.

Matthew Boulton gave financial help to some cartel members who then purchased Boulton & Watt engines. His fortunes were further bound to Cornwall's as a purchaser of copper to use both at the foundry and for the manufacture of coins at his Soho Mint. In order to maintain Boulton & Watt's superiority in Cornwall, Murdoch's role was to keep their engines running smoothly and with as little interruption as possible. Moreover he had to see whether there were any violations of their patents and even for a time report back to his employers if they required evidence for legal action against any infringements by other engineers who included such famous names as Hornblower, Trevithick, Bull and Arthur Woolf. Mine owners were also obliged to pay royalties to Boulton & Watt based on an assessment of coal consumption compared to older, less efficient engines. The task ahead of Murdoch was therefore a complex one. He went there as an engineer but discovered that far more was expected of him. He was responsible for the engines themselves; his were to be the eyes and ears of the company and he found himself in the firing line when the miners felt their work was being impeded.

It was essential that the pumping engines functioned efficiently and economically to allow each mine owner to compete with his rivals. Not surprisingly other engineers, on seeing the success of the Watt engines, were tempted to adopt design features which should have been protected by Watt's 25-year patent. Legal action concerning the patent continued with Murdoch being required to give affidavits in London which he often regarded as a waste of time. Nor was he comfortable with some of these cases and at one point laboured 'under mortal apprehensions that there will be no safety for him in Redruth' if he took an affidavit against one of the mine owners.

Murdoch proved himself capable of dealing with physical violence which occasionally broke out among this volatile workforce. Watt described how Murdoch, beset by several mine captains attempting to 'rag the new boy' took off his jacket and gave 'a bare-fisted drubbing to more than one' of them in 'a lesson of persuasive efficacy ... such as he was never called on to repeat.' He was in Cornwall during the Poldice riots in

1789 when feelings over the price of copper ran high and the miners suffered great financial losses when production was stopped. Thomas Wilson, a major shareholder and agent of Boulton & Watt, told how the miners, asking why their Poldice Mine had been stopped one morning, were advised by the mine captains to ask Murdoch whereupon 'four or five hundred men had gone to his house, taking him out of his chamber and conducted him to the mine for to throw him into one of the shafts, but that he had got clear from them.' Wilson's son described how he himself went through the mine 'five minutes after Murdoch was released, and (met) the whole of them but they said ... they would kill my father if ever they caught him.'

James Watt was all too aware of the danger surrounding Murdoch since he himself had supervised this work before being forced to leave for the sake of his health. Watt wrote to Murdoch expressing their concern 'to learn the jeopardy you were put in by the machinations of these rascals ... Notwithstanding that we feel very much for the uneasiness you must have suffered while in the custody of these villains, we rejoice that you got off without other injury, but shall be anxious till we learn that it has had no bad effects on your health.' The following week, Watt again wrote to Murdoch 'We think that you should not stay at Redruth but at Truro or Saint Austle until these rogues are quieted and take care not to be in their way at night ...' Watt's son later suggested Murdoch be given protection since he was 'a very honest ingenious man and has done some service to the mines, (and) we are persuaded that you will with us, think he is entitled to protection and favour ...'

Inevitably the hostility directed towards Murdoch as he sought to protect his company's interests made its mark and Wilson again wrote 'Murdoch is extremely low very unwell, he complains grievously of the insults he meets with from the men and even children; and is at present very much disposed to leave the county.' In those days the government reacted decisively to any signs of civil unrest, fearing a repeat of events in Paris a few years earlier. Murdoch was not brought back to Soho and as the army was brought in to try to control the angry miners, he and his men loyally maintained their many engines and associated pumping gear.

However, by all accounts he became greatly liked and respected, at times hailed as a hero when his engineering prowess saved the day. On one occasion he is said to have been 'carried home upon the miners' shoulders in triumph' after successful completion of an engine repair.

During the 1778-1782 war with France, Murdoch was advised by his employers to steer clear of press gangs and had been given a letter to summon help should he ever be called into service. In January 1781 an incident occurred which showed him behaving very much as part of the team. At this time privately owned armed vessels were authorised by the French government to take part in the war. One such privateer had sent out a small boat to intercept a vessel carrying Boulton & Watt cargo bound for the Pool mine. Having sailed down the Bristol channel the vessel had reached Portreath on the Cornish coast when it became the target of French sailors attempting to board and carry the cargo to France. The miners who had been awaiting arrival of the cargo opened fire and despite coming under attack by broadsides from the French support ship managed to fight off the attackers from their vantage point at the lighthouse. Watt received word of this incident in a letter from his agent who reported 'Wm. Murdock was one of the people that fired.'

Although his safety was far from guaranteed, especially during the 1790's when great antipathy arose between Boulton & Watt and their rivals over patent rights, he survived many dangers and threats and remained loyal to his employers, often working for days at a time without sleep. His value to the company is obvious from correspondence between the partners, Boulton writing that 'Murdock seems indefatigable ... everyone seems helpless in comparison of him.' 'We want more Murdocks, for of all others he is the most active man and best engine erector I ever saw ... when I look at the work done it astonishes me and is entirely owing to the spirit and activity of Murdock who has not gone to bed three of the nights ...'

And so Murdoch continued to ensure the success of Boulton & Watt in Cornwall, often applying his own

design modifications in order to improve the performance of Watt's engines. In 1796 he fell from a scaffolding
and broke two ribs, but five days later journeyed to
London to assist in yet another court case for Boulton &
Watt. Despite all the controversies over patent rights,
Murdoch remained on good terms with many of the
mine owners and engineers who put his sense of loyalty
to the test on more than one occasion with tempting job
offers. He was offered but did not accept a partnership
with mine owner John Budge a year after going to
Cornwall. Murdoch occasionally managed to find time
to carry out extra work on his own behalf and became
an Adventurer (shareholder) in some of the mines.

Despite company rivalry, Murdoch seems to have
remained on friendly terms with Richard Trevithick although the two men did not have the opportunity of
working together. Redruth renamed his home in Cross
Street 'Murdoch House' which bears a plaque to his
memory and the town holds an annual Murdoch weekend in June to celebrate the life of their beloved engineer and inventor who made his home there for almost
twenty years. In June 2004 there will be a Grand Exhibition to mark the 250th anniversary of his birth. Murdoch's close affinity with the Cornish people might
have had its roots in an ancient kinship shared between
Iron Age people in south-west Scotland and Cornwall.
In the second century AD, the Dumnonii tribe inhabited
both areas of Britain separated by at least seven other
ancient kingdoms. Perhaps even after the passage of
centuries some similarities of character remained and
helped forge a mutual understanding and respect.

7
Murdoch's Steam Carriage

A fool sees not the same tree that a wise man sees
William Blake

In 1782, whilst living in Cornwall, William Murdoch began to ponder on ways of producing locomotion using energy generated by steam. Although his work as manager allowed little spare time, he made frequent trips on foot between the mines and perhaps these walks gave his imagination space and time to come up with ideas. Until now, the steam engine was a stationary beast, mainly used for pumping water out of the mineshaft.

Murdoch, however, knew that machines could be designed to transport people, having worked on and enjoyed riding his father's 'wooden horse' years earlier. He was about to conceive a way to harness the power of steam and transfer energy generated by the piston to turn wheels.

To our minds the step seems an obvious one but with the technological limitations at the end of the 18th century it was a step not yet taken. Until this time, the wheel played only a passive role in locomotion, either horse-drawn or pushed by men. Requiring not just the idea, steam locomotion only became a reality at the hands of a skilled mechanic and Murdoch was the man to combine both of these with a steady conviction that his invention would become the transport of the future.

By 1784 his first working model was seen drawing a small wagon around a room in his house in Redruth. He famously tried out his nineteen-inch long, three-wheeled model one dark evening along the narrow, hedge-lined country lane leading to Redruth church.

Running after his carriage, William was left behind as it accelerated to a speed of 8 mph. Suddenly he heard cries out of the darkness: the rector had been making his way down the lane when he heard an unearthly puffing and snorting and saw the eerie glow of firelight coming towards him. Believing himself in the presence of the Evil One, the unfortunate rector was seized by sheer terror!

Murdoch's steam carriage became familiar to the people of Redruth, especially out on the rough roads at night when it was illuminated by gas lights fixed to its frame. These were constructed from bladders filled with coal gas which was released and ignited in jets issuing from an attached pipe (see p 54). On this first model locomotive, now in the new Birmingham Museum of Science & Discovery, a connecting rod drove a crank forged centrally on the rear axle, the earliest known 'grasshopper' type of working beam. A vertical, double-acting, reciprocating piston operated on a strong-pressure, expansive-working, non-condensing cylinder to move the beam. The engine-beam struck the piston-valve shoulder and a spherical nut on its extension spindle thus operated the piston valve. This model was shown in the 1851 Great Exhibition where it attracted much attention.

Sadly the enthusiasm and excitement with which the people of Redruth greeted his invention was not a response echoed elsewhere. In March 1784, James Watt received a letter from his agent Wilson which referred to Murdoch's carriage. He wrote 'He has got an amazing genius and I am almost afraid will lead him too far, he has mentioned to me a new scheme which you may be assured he is very intent upon, but which he is afraid of mentioning to you for fear of your laughing at him, it is no less than drawing carriages upon the road with steam engines ... he says that what he proposes is dif-ferent from anything you ever thought of, and that he is positively certain of its answering and that there is a great deal of money to be made by it ...'

Almost five weeks later, Watt replied saying he did not foresee much difficulty in moving the carriage by steam but that he was concerned about the weight of boiler fuel and water as well as the inconvenience of obtaining water. He went on '... I esteem that thing certainly possible and practicable, whether profitable or not I am doubtful considering the great expense attending the new schemes ... Mr Boulton will converse with William about it when he comes down to Cornwall till then it had better sleep.'

Over the next few weeks William became anxious to show his steam carriage to Boulton. So dispirited was he by the lack of support from Soho he began to talk of returning home to Lugar. Boulton did travel to Cornwall where he talked to William about the carriage, concluding that the idea was 'a family madness. His father and him were (talking) about one with a corn engine some years ago.' He was also concerned that William was being paid by others to erect engines over and above his wage of £75 a year and since he had saved money and was about to marry a mine captain's daughter, Boulton feared they would be unable to persuade him to agree to stay 'unless we could accomplish it by a side wind.' He suggested the company enter into an agreement with William to make or try to make wheel carriages and to do nothing else but Cornish business for Boulton & Watt. He later wrote to Watt that he thought William 'would sooner give up all his Cornish business ... than be deprived of carrying the (steam carriage) into execution. When a man is mad in any way it is in vain to reason with him about his disorder.' He described how Murdoch feared someone else might take out a patent and suggested to Watt that it may 'be prudent to specify the application of it to wheel carriages without making any drawings. I propose this by way of taking possession and saving the expense of a patent.'

This short-sighted handling of what could have ranked as one of the company's greatest achievements seems astonishing in an entrepreneur of Boulton's experience. But the company's main focus was the Watt engine which, although highly rewarding, required a great deal of attention to in order to maintain its superior status in a fiercely competitive environment.

In a move which Murdoch must have found difficult to understand, Watt agreed with Boulton and failed to take advantage of his protégé's ingenuity, leaving the way open for others to reap the rewards. Having taken out the patent as suggested (although not to oppose Murdoch but to 'stop the gap against wolves and wasps'), Watt forewarned that the machine would be 'clumsy and defective and that it (would) cost much time to bring it to any tolerable degree of perfection ...' He also expressed a fear that the steam carriage would take up Murdoch's whole attention 'to the neglect of more material business' and that if he succeeded they would 'lose the benefit of his knowledge and experience in (their) Cornish business.' In this long letter, Watt set out various ideas for keeping Murdoch on board and at the same time not risking money 'at the directions of a man over whom (he) may not have a proper control and in a scheme (he does) not entirely approve of ...'

Around September 1786 Murdoch was on his way to the patent office with his carriage when he was met by Boulton who attempted to persuade him to give up thoughts of patenting his invention and return to Cornwall. Here Boulton was treated to a demonstration of the carriage when Murdoch had it travel 'a mile or two' in a circle around a room 'making it carry the fire shovel, poker and tongs.'

Courtesy of The National Trust for Scotland

Replica Model
Steam Carriage

Frustratingly all letters to and from Murdoch on this subject are missing from the archives and so his attempts to have his design accepted and his feelings at seeing such an opportunity slip can only be imagined. Less than two weeks after Boulton had seen the carriage for himself, Watt wrote to tell him how he wished Murdoch would 'mind the business in hand and let such as Symington and Sadler throw away their time and money.'

Thanks to inaccurate comments a hundred years or so later, many believed that this was the end of Murdoch's work with steam locomotion. Far from it. Refusing to be discouraged, he constructed a second model this time replacing the 3/4 inch diameter cylinder of the first model with a cylinder of one inch diameter. Murdoch hired an apprentice in 1788 and appears to have gone on to construct at least two further carriages.

By now other engineers began to show an interest in Murdoch's steam carriage. His son John later wrote 'the model of the steam engine with one inch cylinder that works double with slide valves was made in August 1791. It is now at the foundry.' John also wrote that 'the model of the wheel carriage engine was made in the summer of 1792 and was then shown to many of the inhabitants of Redruth - about two years after Trevithick and A. Vivian called at my father's house in Redruth … My father mentions … that on that day they asked him to show his model of the wheel carriage engine which worked with strong steam and no vacuum. This was immediately shown to them in a working state.'

So we know that the young Richard Trevithick was shown the wheel carriage and is likely also to have seen the 3/4 inch cylinder model kept in Murdoch's house. Trevithick would therefore have been aware of Murdoch's early high-pressure, non-condensing locomotive engines when he designed his Whitehead-built model of 1797, now in the Science Museum in South Kensington beside a replica of Murdoch's first model.

During these years, Murdoch had married and experienced the loss of twins, the birth of his two surviving sons and the death of his father-in-law as well as the tragedy of his wife's death. Through such trying times he carried on his work for Boulton & Watt and although he must have felt profoundly disappointed at their lack of support for what he knew to be a hugely significant invention, his loyalty and nobility of character stood the test enabling him to go forward to even greater things. Nor was this loyalty misplaced: James Watt, revered by Murdoch from an early age, was to become a friend and the esteem in which Murdoch was held, not only because of his contribution to science and engineering but also through his association with Boulton & Watt, earned him a place in history despite later attempts to diminish his achievements.

Murdoch appears to have stopped working on his steam carriages around the mid 1790's and on Christmas Eve 1801, Trevithick's first engine was given its trial to great local excitement and it was he who enjoyed acclaim as his engines became familiar sights on British streets. It should not be forgotten that the first model and full sized traction engine had been built in France over thirty years earlier by Cugnot although his work ceased after the engine capsized in a busy street. Happily, William Murdoch lived long enough to see steam carriages and buses carry passengers in London and Glasgow. In the year before his death, the technical revolution reached new heights both in marine engineering and with the launch of Stephenson's Rocket. The steam railway had been born.

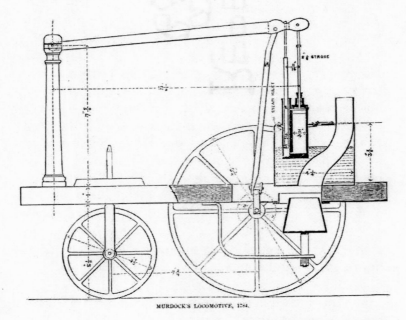

MURDOCK'S LOCOMOTIVE, 1784.

Murdoch's Locomotive, 1784

The Engineer

8
Invention of Gas Lighting

You can see what a great reward for the action lies in just
doing it, that anything honourable has enormous power to
attract the minds of men, that its beauty floods the spirit,
enchants it and seizes it with wonder at its light and radiance.

Seneca

The word 'gas' was first used in the mid 17th century by
Jan Baptiste Van Helmont who, while heating wood in a
retort, realised that not all its vapours could be condensed and there was always a permanent 'wild spirit'.
Taken from the Greek *khaos* (formless), the name has
remained in use ever since. Over the next century
people began to notice coal gas could be ignited but it
took the unique mind of William Murdoch to see it as
more than a scientific curiosity. Realising the potential of
gas light, he carried out a series of experiments and
devised a way to use his knowledge. Only then did gas
lighting become a reality.

Murdoch himself wrote 'at the time I commenced
my experiments I was certainly unacquainted with the
circumstances of the gas from coal having been observed by others to be capable of combustion, ... but ... I
believe I may, without presuming too much, claim both
the first idea of applying, and the first actual application
of this gas to economic purposes.'

Who knows what thought he might have given to
gas light in the years following his boyhood observa-

tions in his mother's kitchen and in his cave by the river? But legend has it that, as he sat smoking his pipe by the fireside in Redruth, Cornwall, he took a tiny piece of burning coal from the fire, placed it inside the

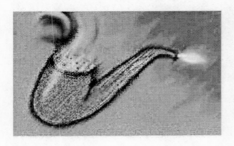

bowl and, having closed the lid, set alight the fine jet of gas issuing from the stem. Once his curiosity had been ignited, he managed to find time despite long working hours and frequent travel between mines, to experiment on the combustible properties of coal, peat, wood and other flammable substances.

He went on to compare coal from different British coal fields and develop means of purifying the gas. Coal was heated in a closed iron retort with carefully controlled air intake and the gas given off conducted a considerable distance through iron pipes or tubes. At intervals along these tubes,

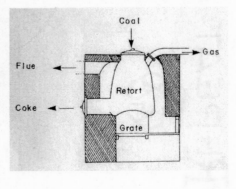

Drawing of a Gas Pot Retort showing how coal is heated to produce gas

William made apertures of various shapes and sizes with the aim of seeing what would give the most efficient and economical results. A few years earlier he had been involved in work with Boulton heating various vegetable and mineral samples in a Papin digester[1] to obtain residues for use in the production of metal. Any accidental ignition of gas during these experiments would have added to William's observations on the quality of light produced not only by coal but other substances. Murdoch had already earned the respect of the people of Redruth who showed great interest in his work. Attention would also have been drawn by the inescapably strong 'rotten-egg' smell of hydrogen sulphide given off when the heated coal came into contact with water during washing.

An old friend of Murdoch's sons recounted many years later the events of one day when Murdoch was carrying out gas light experiments in his workshop in the presence of his friend, the surgeon Dr Boase. Not unusually some boys had gathered outside hoping to witness the strange goings on. One of them was sent by Murdoch to go and bring back a thimble. Returning with the thimble he entered the workshop and became witness to the wonders that followed. Murdoch made small perforations in the crown of the thimble which he fixed to a small pipe. He attached this pipe to the apparatus containing heated coals then lit the gas which burned in steady jets as it escaped through the holes made in the thimble.

[1] One late 17th c. high-pressure machine by Denys Papin digested bones at high temperature giving gas, later used for ballooning. Papin also realised condensed steam would create a vacuum and improve steam engine design.

As gas is being produced from burning coal, so also are tar and other by-products, some of which contaminate the gas, so Murdoch set about finding the best method of washing the gas, a process that resulted in the offensive odour mentioned above. Remarkably he found a way to remove this smell altogether but the remaining gas had lost most of its power to produce light and so he eventually settled on the use of quicklime as the most satisfactory solution. Modern North Sea gas currently in use in the UK has no natural odour and so a noxious smell is added to alert our senses in the event of a gas escape. Similarly in North America, methyl mercaptan is added to gas to produce an offensive smell not unlike decomposing flesh and rotting cabbage!

Murdoch's work with gas light, at this time unknown outwith the small remote community in West Cornwall, further held his neighbours spellbound when he would venture out on a dark night carrying a gas-filled bladder with a pipe stalk tied securely to the opening. Lighting the gas jet, he then went on his way carrying under his arm his ingenious prototype of a mobile gas lamp. This was also the method used at night to illuminate his steam carriage (see p 42).

One dark winter's night a few years later he was about to walk with a friend, William Fairbairn, over uneven roads in Manchester. To light their way he filled a bladder (which he carried with him) with gas from the gasworks, placing it under his arm like a bagpipe. Fair-

bairn wrote admiringly about the incident, concluding that they were able to walk in safety to Medlock Bank. Murdoch adapted this idea for use inside his house by fitting a nozzle to a tinned iron container filled with gas.

Having carried out sufficient tests and refinements, Murdoch, possibly as early as 1792 but certainly no later than 1794, took the defining step of illuminating his own house with gas light. Situated seventy feet from his workshop in Cross Street, the house was well away from any toxic fumes that might escape the retort.

Home of William Murdoch
Cross Street, Redruth

To carry the gas supply inside, he brought an iron pipe (designed and manufactured by himself) from the retort, up through a hole in the window frame and into the house. Having already decided on the best methods of producing the flame, he fashioned apertures at suitable points along the pipe and attached the burners.

Incredibly this momentous invention remained without a patent despite Murdoch's numerous pleas to his employers. On a visit to the Soho works in 1794, he

55

described the process, but although impressed, Boulton and Watt decided not to pursue his invention since they were involved in legal action concerning Watt's steam patent and chose to dismiss any new work that might shift attention away from the firm's main work. Murdoch was aware that Watt's condenser patent would expire in 1800 and predicted correctly that the firm would need a new focus. His frustration at being denied the opportunity to patent and develop gas lighting was therefore not only personal but also because he could see how vital this venture could be to the company's survival in the coming years. Nevertheless, for reasons of their own, Boulton and Watt again failed to take advantage of this golden opportunity just as they had with his steam carriage invention ten years earlier.

With so much to offer and for a man of William's prodigiously creative spirit, such obstruction must have been a cruel blow. A co-partnership in the firm had been discussed but did not materialise and Murdoch began to see the only way to pursue his wishes would be outwith the constrictions of duty to the company. Back in Cornwall the mine owners tried to entice him to work solely for them for a salary of £500 a year but Murdoch decided to leave England and return to his native village. It is believed he started a foundry at Old Cumnock where he erected gas making equipment. The village did not have gas lighting until 1837 and so any work he began was probably discontinued when he left Scotland. If he had chosen to remain, this part of rural Ayrshire might well have become famous as the birthplace of the gas lighting industry as well as the inventor.

9

Return to Soho — Birth of an Industry

Courtesy of Avery Berkel

New Soho Works
Site purchased by W&T Avery Ltd in 1896
now Avery Berkel

Mystery surrounds the activities of William Murdoch while in Scotland. Did he in fact continue to develop gas lighting or did he make further improvements to his steam carriage? No records have yet been uncovered to show how far his work proceeded or why he decided to return to Birmingham. But in 1798 he was made manager of the new Soho works in Birmingham for which he received an annual salary of £1000 and he pressed ahead with the development of gas lighting. March 1802 saw the first public display of gas lighting when the Soho building was illuminated by over 2,600 gas lights in celebration of the Peace of Amiens.

Having completed the illumination of the Soho works, he installed gas lighting at the Manchester house of George Lee and between 1805 and 1807 the cotton spinning mill of Phillips & Lee in Salford was successfully illuminated at a cost of between £5000 and £6000. Lee's later account to a Parliamentary Commission of the comparative cost of the new system confirmed Murdoch's calculations: he stated 'the cost of gas was not more than 50% of that of oil and 70% of the cost of tallow while the light obtained was much more brilliant, much steadier and cleanlier in use.'

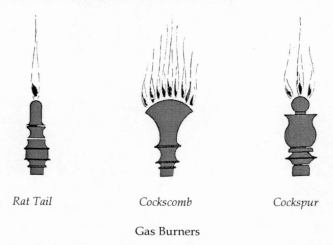

Rat Tail	*Cockscomb*	*Cockspur*

Gas Burners

William Murdoch built gas-producing equipment to be installed in towns and cities but it was not until 1826 that Birmingham installed street lighting. The home of a coppersmith in the Scottish border town of Kelso is said to have been an early convert to gas lighting. One of the first cities to embrace the new technology was Glasgow where booksellers Lumsden, bakers

Hart and the Pollockshaws Auldton Spinning Mill were using gas light by 1805. The Glasgow Gaslight Company was formed in 1817. Concerned about steam (water is a by-product of gas combustion) clouding the inside of the glass globes, the company decided to fit smaller globes which would become hot and so prevent water droplets condensing. What they failed to foresee became all too apparent when the globes shattered as soon as cold raindrops fell on them during the next Scottish shower! No doubt they reverted to large globes.

As this new venture at Soho was in progress at the start of the century, others had begun their own demonstrations of gas light. James Watt's son Gregory, on seeing a public demonstration in Paris of Philippe Lebon's gas thermolamp, anxiously urged his father to delay no further with a patent for Murdoch's idea and appliances. Another witness to Lebon's displays was Friedrich Winzer who changed his name to Frances Winsor and crossed the channel to set up the National Light and Heat Company, performing flamboyant displays of his own in an effort to impress potential investors.

Meanwhile Winsor's solicitor had written to George Lee asking for details on the use of gas lighting within his mill. Lee responded by asking whether the firm intended to do justice to Murdoch's invention, and by informing Murdoch of the proposed company's interest in his work. Winsor applied to Parliament for a Royal Charter of Incorporation and when the Bill was presented to the House of Commons in 1809 Parliament was petitioned in William's name to reject it. William's letter to MPs stated that it was he who first discovered the application of gas as an 'economical substitute for oils and tallow in the production of light.' He also dismissed issues concerning cost and safety of his methods, pointing out that Boulton and Watt had been cautious and judicious in making progress with this system and compared it to their successful steam engine. Appearing before the committee, Murdoch was supported by counsel Lord Brougham who skilfully exposed the folly of Winsor's claims. The difficulty people had in imagining the concept of gas lighting was expressed by an incredulous committee member who asked 'Mr. Murdock, do you mean to tell us we can have a light without a wick?' William was confident that the Bill would be defeated and it was in its third reading in June 1809. Winsor's company had to accept a revised Bill covering only parts of London and with reduced capital.

Struggling to win customers, the company installed gas lighting free of charge in order to advertise its use. Only when Murdoch's assistant, Samuel Clegg, was appointed chief engineer did Winsor's company, now known as 'The London and Westminster Chartered Gaslight and Coke Company' become successful, Clegg replacing Winsor's apparatus with a new plant in the style of Murdoch's at Soho. Gas in the capital was expensive but after 1813 Londoners gradually accepted what a few years earlier could not be given away freely.

As a consequence of some of the fanciful claims

about gas or simply an inevitable part of resistance to change, a temporary climate of opposition even ridicule beset the educated classes. London satirical wit had a field day with chemist Sir Humphry Davy asking whether the dome of St Paul's was to be used as a gas holder. He received the surprising reply that it would take something larger to contain London's gas supply. Another eminent scientist, Wollaston, thought they 'might as well try to light London with a slice of the moon.' Sydney Smith and Sir Walter Scott also enjoyed what they at first took to be the absurd notion of gas-light, Scott painting a picture of 'carrying light under the street in pipes' and 'lighting London with smoke.' Scott, who later visited Murdoch, was however one of the first to have gas light installed in his own home. Glasgow had its own nonsense rhyme:

We thankful are that sun and moon
Were placed so very high
That no tempestuous hand might reach
To tear them from the sky.
Were it not so, we soon should find
That some reforming ass
Would straight propose to snuff them out,
And light the world with Gas.

10
Murdoch's Gift to the World

Initial resistance to the idea of gas lighting was overcome and the social consequences soon proved far reaching. People could now read by the steady, bright gas light instead of straining their eyes using oil lamps or tallow and without ruining their books with dripping candle grease. New worlds opened up, especially for the poor who became more aware of world events by reading an increasing amount of newspapers and pamphlets. Social gatherings on winter evenings became possible; political meetings were popular at halls across the country and of course people could walk home through illuminated streets.

Courtesy of
The National Trust for Scotland

In 1823 in London, a House of Commons Committee declared that '... much benefit would derive from the general introduction of (the use of gas) to light the streets of this metropolis.' As its contribution to the reduction of crime was realised, it was noted that twenty bushels of (gaslight) would have been worth more than many cauldrons of sermons, since burglars would be 'afraid and ashamed to be wicked when light was looking at them.'

Although some people still maintained that the new illumination was
better suited to factories than to
homes, the majority of sceptics were
gradually won over to the idea of gaslight. Sydney Smith, in Epicurean
style, later declared it was 'better to eat
dry bread by the splendour of gas than
to dine on wild beef with wax candles.'

Over the next few decades, gas lighting reached
across the UK to Europe and throughout the civilised
world, catalysing profound changes in society and pav-
ing the way towards the twentieth century and the
dawn of electric light. In the words of Professor Barr at
the presentation in 1896 of a gas engine to Glasgow
University as tribute to the inventor, 'Murdoch was one
of those characteristic inventors who were never satisfied with anything which had been attained, and that,
had he been with (us) that day as one of (our) leading
engineers, without the slightest doubt he would have
been one of the very first, as well as the most hearty, to
adopt the newer and superior mode of illumination
(electricity).'

Following presentation of Murdoch's paper to the
Royal Society on his 'application of the illuminating
properties of carburetted hydrogen gas to the purpose
of furnishing a new and economical light', he was
awarded in 1808 the Rumford gold medal, as 'the
author of the most important or useful discovery which
shall be made published … in heat and light.'

Inscribed *Ex Fumo Dare Lucem* (to give light from smoke), the medal was later melted down and made into a snuff box. This box was exhibited by Murdoch's namesake and grandson at the unveiling of a marble bust in the Hall of Heroes at Stirling's Wallace Monument in July, 1892. Created by Edinburgh sculptor DW Stevenson, this can still be seen positioned between Robert Burns and James Watt, under the watchful eye of the great 16th century preacher, John Knox and opposite King Robert the Bruce. The bust was unveiled by Lord Kelvin who reminded those gathered that although gas lighting was the most known of his inventions, Murdoch also invented coal tar products including the aniline dyes which formed a very large part of the gas works' profits. Lord Kelvin, to the amusement and agreement of his audience, also declared his belief that 'just as gas had succeeded without snuffing out the sun, the moon and the planets, so electricity would succeed without snuffing out gas.'

Lord Kelvin later referred to the statue as one of the perennial memorials of men who had done great things for Scotland. 'Murdoch' he said 'had done great things for the whole world.'

Had Murdoch been motivated by fame and fortune he might well have settled into a long and comfortable retirement on the proceeds of his invention. But his energies were directed towards his work and not toward securing personal gain although he had done all in his power to persuade his employers of the importance of obtaining a patent in the early stages.

William Murdoch

DW Stevenson

Hall of Heroes
National Wallace Monument

It was left to those who followed to express dismay at the lost opportunity to capitalise on this potentially most lucrative of new industries. One hundred years after the invention of gaslighting, his great-nephew, Alexander Murdoch of Glasgow, produced his Sketch of William Murdoch *Light Without A Wick* in which he wrote:

> It is certainly surprising that the man to whom belongs the supreme merit of applying gas to economic purposes, thereby establishing his title to be called one of the age, and who, in addition, was the pioneer of steam locomotion, both on land and sea, should not have had his great services appropriately recognised. Other and smaller men have had monuments erected to their memory all over the country. Indeed, it almost seems as if the fact of his not having patented his gas-lighting invention, which laid mankind under such weighty obligations, and which, with patent rights, would have brought him in a princely fortune, is the main reason why he is so little heard of.

In the summer of 1809 with the company in the hands of Boulton's and Watt's sons, the stage was set for them to dominate the gaslight market as it had the steam market. Just as William's ideas to produce small steam engines were not taken up by Boulton & Watt so were the market opportunities for small scale gas lighting installations neglected. This was unfortunate since the demand for gaslight by shopkeepers and small industries was great indeed. The company therefore left the way open for competitors to exploit the market.

Once he had developed his invention to the stage of mass production Murdoch's interest needed to be aroused by further new fields. If asked, he could have become involved in solving issues such as large scale storage and distribution of gas. He was a man who enjoyed technical challenges and so his would have been the ideal mind to have found the best solution to these new problems. But by 1814 no more was required of him and he ceased to be involved in the gas industry.

11
Murdoch the Man

The honest heart that's free frae a' Intended fraud or guile,
However fortune kick the ba' Has aye some cause tae smile.
Robert Burns

From the archives, although most of his personal correspondence is missing, it is possible to glean valuable insight into the man Murdoch was, what influenced his values and how he lived his life.

Born a contemporary of Robert Burns (whose tutor was John Murdoch 1747 - 1824), outside influences were few and his role models were neighbours and family. We know from a letter written by a Cumnock resident to the *Glasgow Herald* that he played the violin as a boy in Lugar. Whether others in his family were

also musical is unknown but village life would have had its soirées and celebrations where local talent would be welcomed as entertainment.

In those days it was customary for fathers to pass on their knowledge to their children while sitting around the fire in the evenings. Ayrshire was noted for the strength of its people and its youngsters would not have been sheltered from lively discussions and stories of courage. William's native talent and inspiring family equipped him well for a creative and productive life but his character was further enriched by powerful outside influences.

The Church of Scotland, with its great reforming preachers following the lead of John Knox, played a central role in society at this time. In 1683 the Church had issued guidance to its clergy that 'fathers of whatever estate or condition ... must be compelled to bring up their children in learning and virtue.' In the year of William's birth (which also saw the abolition of the Witchcraft Act) a new Kirk had replaced Cumnock's old pre-Reformation building as the congregation rapidly increased under the ministry of Dr. John Muir, a man who greatly influenced the people of his parish persuading many to abstain from heavy drinking and encouraging 'children of promise'.

Many of the Scots clergy were also politically active. Muir himself had been held prisoner as a Jacobite sympathiser in his native Dunbar and his close friend the Rev. Dr. John Witherspoon of Paisley was the only cleric to sign the Declaration of Independence in 1776.

Such a climate of moral and spiritual conviction played no small part in shaping the Scots character and young William, although likely to have attended the more moderate Auchinleck Church with the Boswells, grew up with sound values which would later help sustain him through times of personal struggle.

Fortune also smiled on William academically since he had the benefit of a lowland Scots education superior to and the envy of the rest of the country. This education system led to the rise of many eminent Scots in all professions, provoking prejudice and hostility amongst some English who, thanks to the oppressive class system, were unused to such freedom of speech and self-expression that were seen to be so much part of the Scots nature. All children were educated together; tenants were encouraged to speak their minds and village life was a breeding ground for religious, political and social debate. Young people therefore tended to grow up with a sense of security and the confidence to explore their potential without fear or inhibition.

Of great importance to youngsters of William's generation was the example set by adults around them: there was need for neither deference nor intimidation between tenant and laird since their relationship was based on a mutual sense of responsibility with both sides knowing 'their place'. Therefore although he came from a comparatively humble background, William Murdoch was well equipped to lead a successful and fulfilling life in any society.

William's father introduced important innovations for his Laird, Lord Auchinleck, and the two men would have spent time discussing improvements and exchanging ideas. Interestingly, Lord Auchinleck continued speaking in mid-Scots after becoming a Westminster MP resisting the trend amongst the gentry to become bilingual (his son, James Boswell, spoke only in English). It was observed that he 'was at no pains to improve his colloquial Scots, which people of fashion would have considered as vulgar, in the beginning of the century.' Ordinary people spoke only in Scots although they were taught to read and write in 'the best English they could muster'.

William himself, although living most of his life in England, may also have retained to some degree his native Scots tongue. It is conceivable that in certain sections of English society Murdoch's accent could have been a stumbling block to acceptance and might in part account for a certain reluctance to acknowledge his work. In 1810 he was called to give evidence at a trial brought by Customs & Excise against the brewery to whom he had sold his idea for making isinglass. Some of his answers were written twice in the court transcript suggesting that people might have had difficulty understanding his dialect and he had to repeat himself. Murdoch was working on an engine in Portsmouth at the time of the presentation on February 25th, 1808 of his paper on gas lighting to the Royal Society. The paper was therefore drafted by James Watt junior (although carefully corrected by Murdoch himself) and presented by botanist Sir Joseph Banks, President of the Society.

However he was obviously a literate man who wrote frequently and appears to have taken considerable pleasure in putting pen to paper. The following three examples demonstrate how his handwriting developed from his early years in Cornwall as a young man of 27 through to his mid fifties when back in Birmingham supervising the new Soho Works. The joyous embellishment of his capital letters in the third example suggests that as he matured he kept alive his native flame of creativity and self expression.

Courtesy of Birmingham City Archives

Address and Signature
Letter to James Watt
May 23rd 1782

TRURO

James Watt Esqr
Soho Foundery —
near
Birmingham

Redruth 23 Septr 1798

Mr Watt

Dear Sir

Yours I received and I am glad
you do not blame me for my absence
from Soho Foundery —— the Engine
one West Mr Jewel mine is set to
work — and I intend to Set Out for
Soho On Friday or Saturday next —

Address and Extract
Letter to James Watt
September 23rd 1798

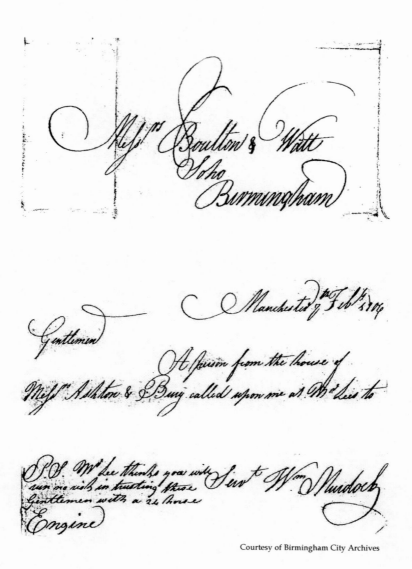

Address, Letterhead and Signature
Letter to Matthew Boulton & James Watt
February 7th 1806

William was privileged to grow up not only with a firm grounding in reading, writing and arithmetic at school in Old Cumnock but also amidst significant agricultural improvement and with a father who thrived on innovation. His native 'freedom of spirit and expression of opinion' existed alongside a steadfast loyalty, traits which were to shape the nature of his relationship with his employers. Throughout the most trying times, he chose to remain loyal to Boulton & Watt even when other opportunities for financial security arose.

He would have been aware of the reasons for his employers' reluctance to patent his steam carriage and gas lighting but, although the sense of frustration at such injustice must have been considerable, he did not allow the subsequent loss of recognition to embitter him. By nature a self-sufficient and highly accomplished individual, his deep sense of commitment to the team, ingrained since childhood, never left him. He valued highly the approval of James Watt who came to respect him and regard him as a friend. Watt later wrote, 'I shall always retain a due sense of the zealous friendship with which you have furthered my views, and the invaluable assistance I have derived from you.'

Murdoch's inventive mind and creative drive led him always towards his next project with absolute commitment. Writer William Buckle described how 'the rising sun often found him after a night passed in incessant labour still at the anvil or turning lathe, for with his own hands he would make those articles he would not trust to unskilful ones.'

He did not toy with ephemeral ideas but used his imagination to produce practical solutions to the problems of his day. Always his father's son, he needed to travel, so he invented the steam carriage; he needed large stone pipes so he invented a machine to make them; he needed his machines to work more efficiently so he designed new gearing mechanisms; he needed light in order to work at night so he invented gas lighting. With a single-minded determination to overcome impediments, his contribution during this exciting period in history was truly astonishing.

Alexander Murdoch later wrote of his great-uncle 'his habits were simple, his nature retiring, his character upright and honourable, modest and unobtrusive to a fault, and the current of his long life comparatively uneventful.' Taking a closer look at what is known of him, a picture emerges of a complex man at times taciturn, at times outspoken; a sensitive man who nevertheless could fight back if he had to; caring and generous but undemonstrative; utterly loyal but committed to his pursuits even when faced with great discouragement and disappointment. He would complain bitterly if he felt his time was being squandered on attending to 'trifles' when he could be occupied with real business. He was once described as being 'all glass' during the difficult days in Cornwall when his anxiety prompted him to ask for deliverance from the place. At times his temper would flare and he would tackle antagonistic Cornish miners by asking them to step outside and settle any dispute head-on.

Not surprisingly Murdoch was intolerant of idleness and incompetence but he did not waste energy bearing grudges. From himself he exacted high standards and expected the same of others. So absorbed was he in whatever project was at hand, his patience quickly wore thin if work was held up for reasons he saw as avoidable. When working away from Soho, he would write to his employers with details of materials required. Any delay in their response prompted a quick reminder from Murdoch who, although polite, made it clear that he was not content to sit back and wait.

Physically he was an impressive figure: strong and muscular, around six foot three inches (1.9m) tall and handsome with a large, well-shaped head and wide, smiling mouth. His hands were ideal craftsman's hands with their strong, spatulate fingers giving a high degree of manual dexterity. As a young man he did not drink alcohol and this gave him an advantage over other employees. He was introduced to brandy when suffering 'ague' which appeared only to aggravate his condition and give him a violent headache. In later years he always kept a plentiful supply of port and brandy which he and his sons shared with guests.

He seems to have had little time for religion and politics and there are no anecdotes to show whether he had a sense of humour although his features suggest a person who was no stranger to laughter. It is easy to imagine that a person with his ability to think laterally would also have appreciated the humourous and he may well have used charm to defuse tricky situations. Perhaps the fact that he set so little store by proving his genius was the very reason his mind remained free to concentrate, enabling him to withstand setbacks and continue to follow whatever course he chose with renewed enthusiasm.

Although he did not profit from his greatest inventions he proved himself indispensable and was eventually raised to a higher status with a considerably increased salary when he returned as manager of the new Soho Works. He was not, however, naïve about money: as an Adventurer he owned shares in some of the Cornwall mines and he later sold one of his ideas for the sum of £2,000. As time went on, he was able to afford to patent his own work and did not need to rely on his employers (the cost of a patent at that time was £40). In 1810 he declined the offer of a partnership when the firm was in the hands of Boulton's & Watt's sons, preferring to earn a fixed salary rather than shoulder liability should the company's fortunes decline.

At the age of 31 William married Anne Paynter, nineteen-year-old daughter of a Cornish mine captain, following a passionate courtship. Anne gave birth to 'frail' twins William and Anne who survived until the winter of the following year when they died within three months of each other. After the burial of his second twin, William himself was very ill but whether from physical causes or from grief is not known. His son William was born in 1788 followed by the birth of his youngest son John two years later. Tragically his wife died shortly wife died shortly after the birth of their second son and the boys were brought up by William and his mother-in-law who moved into the family home for a time. The boys also spent time with their grandparents at Bellow Mill from where they attended Ayr Academy. Following the death of his mother, William wrote to James Watt from the family home at Bellow Mill on June 30th, 1800 thanking him for his kind letter (presumably of condolence). His father died in 1806, just two years before William received the Royal Society gold medal.

Letterheading

William Murdoch
to James Watt
from
'Below Mill'

William had often put his life at risk in pursuit of his work, clambering amongst hot engines that belched forth scalding steam and descending to the depths of mineshafts to repair equipment. He suffered two serious accidents: the first was at the age of forty-two when he broke two ribs falling from scaffolding. In 1815 while working in Leamington, a heavy iron casting crushed his leg above the ankle and he had to face a two-month enforced recuperation period as well as the threatened amputation of his leg. Fortunately he recovered but the injury might have left him with a limp. Shortly after returning to Soho (by water to cushion the pain of travelling) he threw himself back into work and was soon coming up with ideas for new Glasgow waterworks*.

----

*For many years the notion of transporting water by gravity from Loch Katrine to Glasgow was ridiculed until Frederick Bateman successfully installed the Manchester service. 26 miles of tunnel and aqueduct were constructed and in 1859, Glasgow first received its water from Loch Katrine which it does to this day. The steamer, Sir Walter Scott, operates on the loch.

He continued working until the age of 76, although he had to contend with serious illnesses, frustrating for someone of his temperament and the cause of increased irritability in later years. He had recurrent bouts of rheumatism, indigestion, headaches and fever, believed to be malaria. At that time malaria was not uncommon amongst miners as disease-bearing mosquitoes could thrive in the moist, warm conditions of the Cornwall tin and copper mines where stagnant pools of water provided the ideal breeding ground for this parasite. He nevertheless bore his afflictions with characteristic fortitude and remained active well into old age.

Courtesy of Avery Berkel

Murdoch's Home at
13 Foundry Row, Soho
(in foreground)
From 1812-1817

Sycamore House, Handsworth
Home of William Murdoch
from 1817-1839

In 1817 he built a handsome new home, Sycamore House, near Soho which unfortunately was demolished in 1927. Pipes were laid over the fields from the foundry for a distance of half a mile to supply the house with gas for heating and lighting. It was here that he installed some of his domestic inventions described in chapter 14.

Following the death of James Watt, he contributed handsomely to the memorial subscription for a bust to be placed in Westminster Abbey. Baron Dupin noted his thoughts on seeing William Murdoch at the grand public meeting in 1824:

> 'Here was to be remarked among the spectators the venerable old man, whose intrepid services I could have wished had also been rewarded by some flattering remarks of public gratitude.'

Following the death of his son William from tuberculosis, William's own health deteriorated and he was looked after by his younger son, John. On November 15th, 1839, William Murdoch died aged 85. He was buried near James Watt and Matthew Boulton in the crypt of the Church of St Mary, Handsworth. The marble bust by Sir Francis Chantrey was placed in the chancel as a permanent   memorial. His obituary in *Aris's Birmingham Gazette* includes the following passages:

> 'To a strong and muscular frame he united a great activity and dexterity, and much energy and capacity of exertion ... Now that locomotive steam engines applied to carriages have become so extensively used, it is proper to record that the first so applied was made by Mr Murdoch ...'

Throughout his life William Murdoch remained true to his nature, neither submitting to nor dominating but respecting those with whom he worked and for this as well as for his incomparable skill he was loved and respected by those who knew him. In the words of colleague, Thomas Middleton, while Watt was looked on with veneration, Murdoch was 'their pride and joy.' Middleton said at interview in later years:

> 'I was his lad, and used to look after his tools and do errands for him and all that. Ah, he was a wonderful man! There will never be anybody like him again.'

IN MEMORY OF
WILLIAM MURDOCH
BORN AT BELLOW MILL IN
THIS PARISH 21ᵗ AUGᵗ 1754
DIED AT HANDSWORTH IN 1839

LIKE MANY OF HIS
COUNTRYMEN IN ENGLAND
HE ROSE TO EMINENCE BY
THE NATIVE FORCE OF HIS
CHARACTER AND BENEFITED
HIS OWN AND OTHER AGES BY
HIS DISCOVERIES IN GAS
AND BY HIS MECHANICAL
INVENTIONS AS THE
ASSOCIATE OF
WATT AND BOULTON

Inscription on Notables' Obelisk
Auchinleck Kirkyard

John Murdoch
1865

83

12
Order from Chaos

Because half a dozen grasshoppers under a fern make the field
ring with their importunate chink whilst thousands of great
cattle, reposed beneath the shadow of the British oak, chew the
cud and are silent, pray do not imagine that those who make the
noise are the only inhabitants of the field.

Edmunde Burke

Meticulous research by William Murdoch's biographer has brought to light the extent of the loss of correspondence between Murdoch and his colleagues. Throughout his life he would have corresponded with his employers not only through an agent but also directly, especially when conveying highly technical information. While living in Cornwall he had been asked to write on issues such as engine design, his steam carriage and the riot which almost cost him his life. His frequent travel to sites away from home would have necessitated a considerable amount of letter-writing, the only method of communication at that time. This is clearly demonstrated by the large number of letters still in existence whether in response to his own, giving instructions or asking for information.

Rather than the estimated hundreds, just over twenty of his letters remain in the archives, strongly suggesting that the vast majority have been carelessly discarded or deliberately removed. Following his death, some of Murdoch's most important work began to be attributed to James Watt by early biographers. Sadly it appears that Watt's son removed documents which he felt would not support his belief in his father's absolute superiority. This surely was unnecessary since Watt's undoubted genius as an inventor and engineer could happily have existed in history as it did in life alongside Murdoch's equal genius.

Murdoch's personal belongings are long since gone; it is not known what happened to his collection of minerals and fossils or his fathers millgearing. One more recent unsolved mystery is the whereabouts of the gas engine presented to Glasgow University 'as a permanent tribute.' Relocated to the new James Watt Laboratories in 1901, the engine remained there until the 1950's or early 1960's. Whether it was subsequently removed from the University intact or dismantled during renovations is unknown. The engine was an 'Otto' type, manufactured by Messrs Crossley Brothers of Manchester. It was a horizontal, single-cylinder engine of four horse power nominal, capable of 9.2 brake-horse power with a double flywheel and it carried the inscription:

NORTH BRITISH ASSOCIATION OF GAS MANAGERS
This engine is erected as a tribute to the memory of
William Murdoch, Inventor of Lighting by Gas
(1792)
23rd November, 1896

The facsimile of a working model steam carriage housed at Sheffield University until a few years ago can no longer be traced. Nor can the few items be found of Murdoch memorabilia once held in the old Boswell Museum in Auchinleck (the new museum contains no exhibits on Murdoch). Although of no great monetary value, the lost items were part of Murdoch's heritage and their disappearance is to be regretted.

In March 2003 James Watt's private possessions, in the care of his descendents since 1900, came under the hammer at auction following the death of Lord Gibson-Watt of Doldowland. The 564 lots fetched a total of £1.9 million, but the only letter included in the sale was one Watt received from his son Gregory aged 15. Therefore it is still unknown whether the few letters in Birmingham City Archives are all that remain of Murdoch's written legacy or whether other documents might yet be found. The modest nature of Murdoch's legacy contrasts sharply with that of the men whose fortunes were intricately bound up with his own. The magnificent Soho House, Matthew Boulton's home, is testament to the life of a successful and prosperous man. Now a museum, the house proudly displays its splendid contents to the world.

Perhaps the time has come to revive plans to build a museum such as that proposed in 1985 by Cumnock & Doon Valley Council. Funding for this new Murdoch Museum[1] at Bellow Mill did not materialise and the plans were abandoned. The desire to ensure that William Murdoch is not forgotten has led to many forms of tribute, most of which can be enjoyed by the public (details in Tourist Guide p122-7).

---

[1]   A model of the museum is on display at the Baird Institute in Cumnock.

In order to understand why the threat of obscurity came to hover over Murdoch's name, it is necessary to question not only the motives of those who acted after his death but also the nature of his relationship with the network of influential men whose attitudes and actions helped determine the course of his life.

At the time of the Industrial Revolution, scientific endeavour focused mainly on subjects of limited technological use such as astronomy, botany and light refraction. It was not so much science that catapulted Britain into its leading role but the work of those empirical mechanics or 'technical designers' such as William Murdoch, Richard Trevithick and Robert Stephenson. The culture of knowledge in which Murdoch was raised was pivotal to the rapid development of technology and the 'appliance of science'. There was a tremendous desire for scientific learning at this time. Indeed one of the most important changes facilitated by Murdoch's gas lighting invention was the growth in evening meetings where ideas on science, politics and religion were voiced. Publication of pamphlets and newspapers brought information to more people than ever before and fuelled the hunger for knowledge generally.

The notion of the humble artisan labouring in the dark while the enlightened scientist pondered aloft in his ivory tower was now becoming a thing of the past. The road between theoretical knowledge and practical invention was increasingly two-way with much greater communication between those who knew the theories and those who did the work.

The British were unique in their ability to apply knowledge to industrial and commercial advantage and it was the growing culture of exchange of ideas that led to Britain's role at the forefront of industry at this time. Societies began to spring up giving greater opportunities for lectures and discussions. Coffee houses and masonic lodges were favourite meeting places and brought about the creation of formal groups such as Birmingham's Lunar Society[2]. However, more important than the formal meeting was the social networking leading to informal exchange of technical information between members.

The role of Freemasonry during the Industrial Revolution is well documented and it is known that a great many leading figures[3] were members of the brotherhood at this time. The Second Degree charge to 'study the hidden mysteries of nature and science' was of great importance to the members of the Lunar Society. As well as entertaining guests in his 'Lunar Room' at Soho House, Matthew Boulton was a genial host who welcomed a great number of people to his home. Moreover he showed a philanthropic concern for the welfare of his employees at the Soho Manufactory in the true tradition of Freemasonry still observed to this day.

Clearly Freemasonry was a force for good since it helped bring order to the somewhat chaotic nature of knowledge and practice. It has not yet been possible to establish whether William Murdoch was a Freemason but research is continuing. His name does not appear on the list of prominent members of the Lunar Society although he did have an association with the Society. His work was probably the subject of much discussion at meetings and it is said that Erasmus Darwin even asked Boulton to build him the first steam carriage.

Tracing back through history, there is circumstantial evidence to suggest that his family might have had connections with Freemasonry. Both William's father and grandfather were gunners in the Royal Artillery, led by the Duke of Cumberland who became the first Royal Grand Master. The family lived only some thirty miles from the Mother Lodge of Scotland at Kilwinning. Had he been a member, John Murdoch's skills as a wheelwright would have earned him a respected position within the order which had its roots in the medieval craft of stonemasonry.

---

2   Some of Britain's most illustrious scientists and industrialists including Josiah Wedgwood and Samuel Galton met monthly around the time of the full moon (in order that their way home was lit by moonlight).

3   Sir Walter Scott, much loved author and poet and a friend of James Watt was a Freemason as was Robert Burns who became Deputy Master at St James's Lodge in Tarbolton. In the 1770's, Erasmus Darwin (grandfather of Charles Darwin) helped found the Lunar Society. He had been initiated at St David's Lodge No 36 in Edinburgh in the year of Murdoch's birth, only four years after the Grand Lodge of the Royal Order of Scotland had been re-constituted. He was Fellow of the Royal Society founded in the seventeenth century by, among others, Freemason Elias Ashmole. Erasmus Darwin's friends included American Freemason Benjamin Franklin, Matthew Boulton and James Watt who was initiated into Freemasonry in 1763, the year he became friendly with John Roebuck, his partner at the Carron Foundry in Falkirk.

In the year 1600, William Schaw, who was known as the creator of modern freemasonry, was accompanied to a hearing at the Palace of Holyroodhouse by John Boswell of Auchinleck, ancestor of Murdoch's laird, Alexander Boswell (Lord Auchinleck). Schaw was Master of Works to the King and Boswell attended not as a member but as clerk to Schaw. It is possible however that Boswell later became a Freemason himself.

Whether or not William Murdoch was a Freemason he would at least have been aware of the benefits of belonging to the organisation. In those early days of travel and social mobility, such membership facilitated progress and led to opportunities for advancement in trade or profession. Perhaps even his initial meeting with Matthew Boulton had been helped along by some sort of introduction from James Boswell.

Speculation aside, Murdoch lived and worked in an environment strongly associated with Freemasonry. His success depended to a considerable degree upon his ability to satisfy the conditions set by his employers whose values and motives were partly shaped by the people they knew. However Murdoch chose to fit into this system, he would not have escaped its influences. From what is known of his nature it seems he made little time for social pursuits, preferring to be at the 'coal face' getting on with the work rather than networking with the great and the good. Could this help explain why he seemed happy to be asked by James Watt junior to remain working in Portsmouth, albeit with Brunel and Maudesley, rather than attend the reading of his paper to the Royal Society? Could his native 'free spirit' that worked so well in his favour have been responsible for a certain reluctance to cultivate social connections? Perhaps those times were not so different from today when the rewards of society sit most comfortably on the shoulders of those who strive to win recognition.

Around fifty years after Murdoch's death, plans to apply to Parliament for public acknowledgement of his services to society bore no results. The following words appeared in the journal *Once a Week*:

> Why was not Murdock rewarded by the Parliament which rewarded Mrs Stevens for a cure which turned out to be no cure at all, and Dr Smyth for *not* inventing fumigation by acids, and Mr Manby for another man's inventions, and Mr Macadam for doing what had been done in Switzerland and elsewhere time out of mind? Ask Parliamentary sapience and justice why. Omniscience can doubtless answer for what omnipotence performs.
>
> But it is all luck. Mr Murdock got no patent, no reward and no fame. 'Known to be the inventor?' 'Yes.' 'To whom?' 'To Messrs. Watt and Boulton and twenty others.' Alas! Fame and fortune are twin impostors, and what the one does the other will not swear to. But thou wert an ignoramus, old Murdock! Why didst thou not puff thyself? Thinkest thou that if Sir A or Sir B had invented the gas light we should ever have heard the last of it?'

1881

Powerful though the institutional machinery of Britain was, it is heartening to know that William Murdoch's reputation has survived the pressures that might have relegated him to perpetual obscurity. Such was the nature of the man, his ability and the significance of his work, he will always be remembered as one who achieved recognition not only as an associate of Boulton and Watt but also by his own merits.

This memorial unveiled by Sir Percy H Mills BT, KBE
September 14, 1956

Commemorates the immense contribution made by
Boulton Watt and Murdoch
to the Industry of Birmingham and of the world.
The conception of Richard Wheatley
a leather goods manufacturer of this city
coupled with his generosity and a contribution by the
City Council enabled these statues to be executed by:

W Bloye
Sculptor

Statue of William Murdoch, James Watt and Matthew Boulton

W Bloye

outside Birmingham Register Office

13
A Fishy Story

In 1786 the London brewery of Messrs. Barclay Perkin & Co. installed a new Boulton & Watt engine. The brewery had previously used water pumped from a well on the site, the pumps operated by horses travelling round and round on a circular platform. This was the single-acting beam engine converted ten years later to double-acting that has recently been refurbished and now operates in its new home at the Royal Museum of Scotland.

Although Murdoch was still living in Cornwall, he had travelled to Scotland in late April, perhaps to introduce his new wife to his family, returning three weeks later via London where he carried out some work at the Albion Mill. Whether then or during another of his visits to London to give evidence at a patent hearing, he is said to have worked on this new engine.

The brewery manager explained to Murdoch they had been having great difficulty in making the beer clear and bright, and asked if he could suggest anything. It seems Murdoch rose to the challenge, buying fish skins from Billingsgate market and taking them back to his 'genteel lodgings'. It is easier to imagine the events that followed if he had been there alone rather than with his wife. With characteristic single-mindedness, he turned his room into a laboratory, spreading fish skins around and experimenting on ways of manufacturing isinglass.

Next morning his landlady discovered these fish skins hanging up to dry on her sitting-room curtains. Horrified at the sight and no doubt shocked by the smell, she ordered him out of the house. He perfected the technique elsewhere resulting in a new isinglass as an alternative to the expensive Russian product made from sturgeon. It proved a splendid success and he was handsomely rewarded by a payment of £2000 from the grateful London Brewers.

Under cross examination at a later trial brought by Customs & Excise against the brewers, Murdoch argued successfully that this was not an additive since it was discarded from the beer along with the impurities which it precipitated. With the help of his evidence and that of renowned Cornish chemist Humphry Davy (who gave his name to the miner's safety lamp), the prosecution case collapsed.

Boulton & Watt Rotative Beam Engine
from Barclay Perkin & Co Brewery, London
now in the Royal Museum of Scotland, Edinburgh

<u>*Horse Power*</u>

Every mechanical engineer knows that James Watt first used the term 'horse power'. The following account by R Barclay Murdoch is from the *Gas Journal* of 1929 and refers to one of the earliest examples of engine power equated to horse power. He wrote:

> Fresh light has been thrown upon an incident in William Murdoch's life with which the writer was acquainted but of which he did not appreciate the significance.

Having told the story of isinglass from fish skins he went on to describe how the manager of Barclay Perkin brewery was curious to know how many horses were equivalent to the power of his new Boulton & Watt engine. Murdoch noted how much work the brewery horses actually had to perform in order to pump a certain amount of water. He then calculated the size of the boiler, pressure of steam and other data necessary to find out what size of engine would be required to perform an equivalent amount of work to that of one horse. This gave him a formula for the now universally adopted 'horse-power' of engines of any kind.

The term was used frequently, Murdoch himself writing to Watt from Glasgow on August 18th, 1802 'Mr Holsworth & Co of Anderston Cotton Mill gives you orders for a 45 or 50 horse engine...' continuing 'Messrs Sterlings printers on the river Leven gives you orders for a 16 or a 20 horse engine with an iron beam cross plate and pillar...' In 1806 Murdoch, while installing the first large-scale gas lighting at Phillips & Lee (see page 58), wrote a letter to Watt which included a PS asking about a 24 horse engine for a new customer who had called to see him.

Two extracts from a letter from
William Murdoch to James Watt
18th August, 1802

'Horse power' appears to have been widely adopted by manufacturers and purchasers of engines but not everyone was satisfied with this definition. According to the Oxford English Dictionary, the first published use of the term was in 1806. In his book, *A Treatise of Mechanics,* Olinthus Gregory of the Royal Military Academy offered his opinion as follows: 'the usual method of estimating the effects of engines by what are called 'horse powers' must inevitably be very fallacious, unless all engineers could agree as to the quantity of work which they would arbitrarily assign to **one** horse, and in that case the term would be nugatory' (to no purpose). This suggests that a consensus had not yet been reached on how to define the work of one horse. Toward the end of the nineteenth century, use of the term was broadened to include electricity but failed to win approval. The *Electrician* stated 'a new and shockingly unscientific unit, the electrical horse power, is insensibly coming into use.' A few years later the *Glasgow Herald* published an article predicting 'the term horse-power has probably seen its best days ... As a scientific term it has been much abused, and as a commercial term it conveys no meaning.'

The problem was that although the term was useful in comparing engines of different size it was inaccurate at defining the actual work done by the engine. In the 1960's, the more specific term 'brake horse-power' was introduced. Calculated by deducting the power absorbed through engine friction from that generated by the cylinder, this described the amount of power actually available. It then became possible to compare engines by the work they did rather than their size alone.

As early as 1760 James Fergusson wrote about horse power in his *Lectures on Mechanics, Hydrostatics and Pneumatics* so the notion of measuring this was not new. Just when engine power was first related to horse power is difficult to establish and, although intriguing, it is of little importance whether the above account of Murdoch's calculation does in fact describe the first time this connection was made.

At a time when so many businesses were changing from horse power to steam power the question would have been a natural one and was probably asked on more than one occasion. If Murdoch, as was his style, took it upon himself to provide an answer he is likely to have passed on the idea to James Watt as he did with so many other ideas. The concept was put to further practical use by Watt in later contracts with Cornish mine owners when royalties were calculated on the number of strokes made by an engine of a particular horse power determined by Watt's formula.

The last man to be concerned with splitting hairs would have been William Murdoch himself. He delighted in coming up with new ideas and seeing them put into practice but he was not possessive about his knowledge. Whether he or someone else was first to associate horse power with engine power, there is little doubt that to see how this simple idea has been developed over two centuries and remains part of everyday language would surely have made him smile.

14
Other Inventions & Innovations

In the culture I grew up in you did your work and you did not
put your arm around it to stop other people from looking—you
took the earliest possible opportunity to make knowledge known.
James Black

William Murdoch's legacy to the world extends to an impressive variety of mechanical and chemical inventions. Not only did he provide some of the finest and most elegant solutions in his main field of engineering, but he showed no inhibition in transferring his energies toward other areas in a manner true to his youthful curiosity and drive. Some of these inventions are categorised below, illustrating his unique grasp of natural and mechanical forces and his skill in harnessing this energy. His reputation was indeed well-deserved. Following a visit made to Soho in 1830, the highly respected engineer, James Nasmyth, wrote:

The admirable genius of William Murdoch made me feel that I was indeed on classic ground in regard to everything connected with the construction of steam-engine machinery. The interest was in no small degree enhanced by coming every now and then upon some machine that had every historical claim to be regarded as the prototype of many of our machine tools. All these had William Murdoch's genius stamped upon them by reason of their common-sense arrangements, which showed that he was one of those original thinkers who had the courage to break away from the trammels of traditional methods, and to take short cuts to accomplish his objects by direct and simple means.

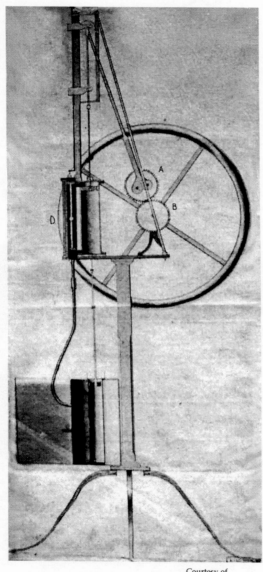

Left

'Murdoch's
Little Engine'
with
Sun and Planet Gear
and
D-Slide Valve
(D)

Right

Detail showing
Sun and Planet Gear
in
Model
Beam Engine
at the Gas House,
Culzean Castle

Sun and Planet Gear 1781

From his early days with Boulton & Watt, William Murdoch introduced many improvements to engine design to the advantage of the company. His terms of employment made clear that his inventions were the intellectual property of his employers and so William's groundbreaking work converting steam power to produce rotary motion thus turning wheels was patented by and attributed to James Watt (who also patented four other methods of rotary motion).

One of Murdoch's finest inventions was his Sun and Planet gear. As Smiles wrote 'eventually (Watt) adopted the Sun and Planet motion, the invention of Murdock.' When James Nasmyth visited Soho in 1830 he too recorded seeing 'the engine with the sun-and-planet motion, an invention of William Murdoch.'

Murdoch devised this method to convert the up and down motion of the rod on the end of the beam to circular motion, first using the technique on the Wheal Maid engine in Cornwall. The Planet (A) was fixed to the connecting rod therefore did not rotate. The up and down motion caused the planet to rotate the Sun (B) which was attached to the crankshaft (C), giving continued or circular motion around an axis. A feature of the Sun and Planet gear was that the crankshaft rotated twice for every revolution of the planet.

103

Replica Model
Oscillating Cylinder Engine
(1785)

Oscillating Cylinder Engine 1785

While working in Cornwall around 1783, Murdoch became enthusiastic about his idea for small engines, and despite lack of interest from Watt, built the first oscillating cylinder engine in 1785, operated by compressed air and later put on display at the Great Exhibition of 1851. Between 1802 and 1828 Murdoch's idea was re-patented four times for use in carriages, locomotives and paddle steamers. His design which incorporated eccentric gearing provided the first alternative to the working beam thus saving space, important in its role in marine engineering well into the 20th century.

Although Boulton & Watt fitted oscillating cylinder engines in around fifty vessels, rival companies cornered the market for large ships and it was a Maudesley twin-cylinder engine that in 1828 was first to power a large ship: the 37-ton *Endeavour* in its first journey between Richmond and Westminster Bridge. Maudesely's designer, Joshua Field, had discussed steamboat design on a visit to Murdoch at his home seven years earlier. One of Field's engines was used in the *Great Western* (designed by the son of Murdoch's friend Brunel) which made the first Atlantic crossing in the year before Murdoch's death. London's earliest passenger carriage built by Hancock which came into service in the same year also used twin oscillating cylinders. There are still some large oscillating cylinder paddle steamer engines in service on the river Weser in Dresden. The earliest one was built around 1856 by John Penn & Co., London and is still going.

Murdoch's
D-Slide Valve

(detail from 1799 patent)

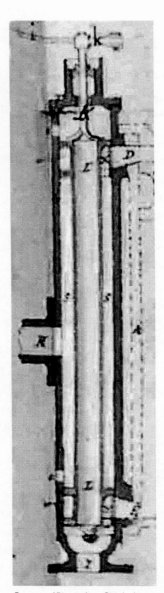

Courtesy of Birmingham City Archives

D-Slide Valve 1799

Murdoch had used a slide valve in his steam carriage of 1784 and continued to develop and simplify this mechanism until 1799 when he applied for a patent in which he wrote: 'I simplify the construction of the steam valve ... (by) connecting the upper and lower valves so as to be worked by one rod or spindle, and in making the stem or tube which connects them hollow, so as to serve for an eduction pipe to the upper end of the cylinder, by which means two valves are made to answer the purpose of ... four.' The valve, in use for many years, took its name from the D-shaped central hollow piston. It eliminated many of the complicated movements of rods and bars and was probably the greatest improvement to the rotative engine since Watt's cylinder with separate condenser.

The patent for Murdoch's D-slide valve also covered two important changes to engine design: the worm-wheel and single-cast steam casings. The latter simplified 'the construction of the steam vessel and steam case ... by casting the steam case of one entire cylinder' within which he placed the working cylinder thus avoiding the need for segmented castings. Since the cylinders were kept hot by steam which filled the space between them this became known as a 'steam-jacketed cylinder.' This casting method was still in everyday use in piston engines almost 200 years later. Such designs illustrate how Murdoch's experience as a pattern-maker combined with his experience in construction to give him a unique advantage over other engineers.

Worm Wheel 1799

This adaptation of the endless screw (invented in 1777 by Jesse Ramsden as part of a machine for dividing mathematical instruments) was also part of Murdoch's patent of 1799. He designed an engine-powered endless screw working into a toothed wheel to produce 'a more steady motion than is obtained by any of the methods now in use.' His method was widely applied to machine tools and for use in the home (see page 114). The worm wheel is non-reversing, making it ideally suited for cranes since the load cannot take over and wind back if the engine stops.

Worm Wheel

Shaft with endless screw (S) to be turned by the 'acting power'
Cogs on toothed wheel (W) contact the screw producing steady motion

Courtesy of Birmingham City Archives

Steam Wheel 1799

In a further development of rotary motion, Murdoch developed a steam wheel (part of his 1799 patent) that overcame problems with current models. Simpler and more practical than Watt's design, this was used to drive machinery at Soho foundry for over thirty years.

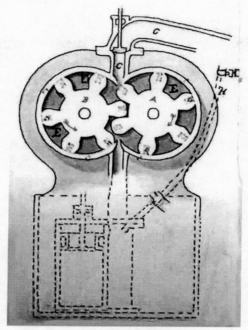

Steam Wheel

Steam enters the cylinder via pipe (C) and is trapped between vanes. As it expands, it turns wheel (A) clockwise and wheel (B) anti-clockwise. This was the simplification that Murdoch patented.

As exhaust steam condenses into the container below, a vacuum is created helping to drive the system. The chamber on the left is an air pump (driven by a crankshaft from the engine) to remove accumulated air and condensed steam as well as injection water introduced via pipe (H) to speed the rate of condensation. A proportion of this water from the air pump is fed back to the boiler while the rest goes to a cooling pond and is recycled to cool the engine in a process developed many years earlier by Thomas Newcomen.

Ventilation Bellows 1781

During the time he was developing his oscillating cylinder engine, Murdoch's long-term fascination with compressed air increased. He designed and constructed bellows to ventilate the Cornwall mines using a rotating drum containing three vanes whereby stale air was compressed as it passed through a water reservoir then forced out through a nozzle allowing fresh air to enter the mine. Murdoch's drawing is headed 'Wm. Murdoch's bellows, made in Cornwall 1781, afterwards in common use among the miners.' Although successful, it does not seem to have been developed further.

Ventilation Bellows

24 inch (0.6m) diameter
20 inch (0.5m) long

Drum rotates forcing
stale air through valves
to water reservoir
and out through nozzle

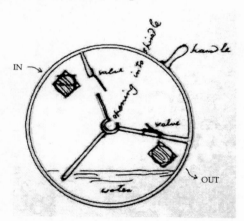

Courtesy of Birmingham City Archives

Bell Crank Engine c. 1799

In the first decade of the 19th century, the steamboat *Clermont* heralded in a new mode of transport when it came into service carrying passengers on the Hudson

River. Its Boulton & Watt engine had been adapted to include a bell crank lever connecting the cylinder to the paddle wheels, a method invented by Murdoch around five years earlier. Murdoch's genius was not confined to steam engine design but spilled over into other areas including machine tools and the utilising of waste materials and energy. Fairbairn noted that in the nineteenth century, 'everything is done by machine tools with a degree of accuracy which the unaided hand could never accomplish.' One of William Murdoch's abiding passions was compressed air used to great effect in the oscillating cylinder engine. His imaginative use of this form of energy gave rise to a variety of engineering and domestic machines.

Compressed Air Pump 1788

This ingenious idea to replace high-friction water pumps in the deep Cornwall mines was made a reality in the spring of 1788 when Murdoch's first (and possibly only) compressed air pump began operation. A short length of 1 inch copper pipe was used to compress the air at the top of a 3 inch (8 cm) diameter pipe running all the way to the bottom of the 40-foot well where the air operated 17-inch pumps. He pulled a string (probably attached to a valve at the bottom) allowing water to be pumped back up to the surface.

It is unknown why this was not developed, although it was probably susceptible to damage, but he returned to the development of wooden pumps. The stirrup pump familiar in the 20th century operated on the same principle.

Pneumatic Lifting Gear 1813-14

In order to save water during the passage of vessels through locks in canals or docks, Murdoch invented pneumatic lifting gear worked by compressed air operating an air-tight vault at the bottom of the lock. In 1827 he lodged a caveat for a patent for this but decided not to oppose the patent application taken out by his friend in Leeds the following year. Unfortunately, the company, under control of Boulton's & Watt's sons, failed to take advantage of an opportunity to install this machinery at St Catherine's dry dock in 1828, despite strenuous efforts by Murdoch and his son William. His pneumatic lifts had been used to great effect from 1798 in the transport of materials from the canal to a series of designated areas at Soho: the drilling shop; heavy turning shop; nozzle shop; fitting shed; parallel motion and working gear shop; light fitting shop; pattern shop; casters' shop and smiths' shop thereby creating what is thought to have been the world's most advanced division of labour with built-in advantages such as increased safety and cost-efficiency. Here he used compressed air from the foundry blower to operate a 10-foot diameter, 12-foot stroke piston. Another application eliminated the need for counter-shafting and belt drives to operate machine tools. Each machine was fitted with a small vacuum piston engine controlled by a central exhauster pump supplied with compressed air from the foundry. A similar system installed by Murdoch was in use for 35 years running lathes in the pattern shop. Later this was in common use in factories to power equipment such as sewing machines.

Pneumatic Doorbell c. 1817

Murdoch installed a pneumatic doorbell at Sycamore House, which he built in 1817. Operated by a column of air in a pipe with glass tubing at both ends, the bell was struck by a knob attached to a piston that moved in response to pressure on the piston at the door. Sir Walter Scott, a friend of James Watt, had seen the air bell at Murdoch's house and had one installed at his own home.

Pneumatic Dispatch Scheme

The transmission of letters and packages through tubes operated by a vacuum created by an air-pump was another of Murdoch's inventions still in use as recently as the 1960's. This was first put into practice by the London Pneumatic Dispatch Company about 1853. The atmospheric railway later developed by a pupil of Murdoch worked on the same principle and was widely used in the first half of the twentieth century.

Steam Cannon 1803

While at Soho, Murdoch built a steam cannon in order to knock down a wall. Its success is unknown but this device was described by William Buckle in 1850.

High Pressure Steam Gun c. 1803

This gun was designed to fire one-and-a-quarter inch (3 cm) lead bullets and the principle was later used as a technique for launching planes from aircraft carriers.

Smoke Jack Wheel c. 1821

Joshua Field (see page 105) described how Murdoch constructed a smoke jack for basting a joint of meat as it roasted at the fire in his kitchen at Sycamore House. Field wrote, 'he has a jack which is like a smoke jack wheel hung just over the meat and turned by the current of air ascending in front of the fire. The most curious part of this jack is the manner of hanging it with little friction. There is a cup of iron above it having another cup in it floating in mercury.'

The smoke jack was placed in the narrowest past of the chimney where the flow of smoke was fastest. The force of the machine depended upon the draught from the chimney and strength of the fire. Pulley jacks were also used for turning a spit. One design incorporated Murdoch's worm wheel with endless screw (see page 108). The descent of a weight, which was wound up by a handle, was controlled by a system of pulleys, the worm wheel ensuring steady rotation of the jack.

Hot Air & Gravity Fed Central Heating c. 1817

Field also records in his 1821 diary that Sycamore House had 'a good stove for heating the rooms with hot air which enters the rooms and staircases at convenient places.' In 1815, two years before the house was built, Murdoch had installed a gravity-fed hot water system to heat Leamington Spa baths using a series of pipes laid throughout the building to circulate water heated by a steam boiler. He later developed this system to circulate steam, a method universally adopted and still in use almost two hundred years later.

Machine for Holing Stamp Grates 1788

In 1788 Murdoch was involved in the design of equipment for Boulton's Soho Mint which struck medals and rimmed coins. While in Cornwall, he invented yet another labour-saving therefore money-saving machine described by Boulton & Watt's agent: 'Murdoch has made a machine for holing stamp grates with which he can do as much for one pence as can be done by hand for six pence and so much superior that he has constant employment for it...'

After mining, tin or copper ore had to be crushed or 'stamped' into fine particles using a heavy steam-driven weight which dropped onto the ore. The crushed ore passed through stamp grates, a series of grading devices with smaller and smaller holes at each stage. Murdoch's machine allowed the holes in the cast iron to be formed with much greater speed and efficiency than ever before.

Pipe Boring Machine 1810

Murdoch had earlier used a machine of his for cutting wooden pipes and it was this that he developed before taking out his final patent in 1810 for cutting stone pipes. Instead of destroying the material from inside the pipe, a cylindrical crown saw cut out a solid core from which a smaller pipe and a smaller core could then be cut. During cutting, a stream of water carried off waste materials.

Iron Cement 1784

It was essential that steam engine joints were made both air-tight and water-tight but only after Murdoch's serendipitous discovery could these qualities be guaranteed. On observing that iron filings in the bottom of his tool bag had been accidentally mixed with ammonium salts and set rock hard, he experimented with this mixture to produce iron cement which Boulton described to Watt: 'the method of using sal ammoniac in the making of joints seems to answer so well that an engine being once well put together may be carried about as one solid piece without spoiling the joints.'

Watt's attempt to improve this cement by the addition of sulphur succeeded in reducing the setting time but contact with steam gave off sulphuric acid which made the compound brittle.

The strength of the joints was due to the irreversible rusting process that set the compound solid and so this cement came to be known as rust cement. When old water pipes are dug up, rust cement is easily identifiable by its reddish-brown colour. Lumps of cement often remain long after the pipe itself has disintegrated.

---

1   Aniline is a toxic, oily substance with a pleasant odour obtained from burning organic material including coal, wood and indigo. It is also used in the manufacture of drugs, explosives, plastics and photographic chemicals.

2   Town gas works, part of which dates back to the year of Murdoch's death in 1839, are preserved at the Gas Works Museum in Biggar (see page 129)

116

Dyes, Paints, Colours & Preservatives 1791

In 1791 William Murdoch had taken out a patent on a method to produce dyes, paints, colours and preservatives from the heating of pyrites (minerals) mined in Cornwall. In his patent he describes how he put the pyrites into a 'kiln, house, oven, cone or heap, covered nearly close, and then set the same on fire, admitting no more air than is sufficient to cause the said pyrites or other material or ores to burn, the fumes or smoke of which must be conducted through a flue or conductor from the top receiver in which the smoke is condensed.'

Although it was some fifty years before coal-tar or aniline[1] dyes were produced commercially, his method of collecting 'fume or smoke' set the scene for his work with gas light. A hundred years later Lord Kelvin pointed out that Murdoch's aniline dyes formed a very large part of a gas works' profits[2].

Throughout his life, Murdoch made valuable investigations into alloys and amassed an impressive collection of minerals and fossils which attracted the attention of amateurs and professionals alike. Wanlockhead is noted for its minerals and his love of mineralogy might have taken hold while there as a young man. During his work with steam engines deep underground in the mineral-rich Cornwall mines, Murdoch would have found many specimens for his collection. His friendship with Gregory Watt, James Watt's son, might have grown from this interest which both men shared.

Jet from Peat Moss

Another invention suggests he might have found naturally-compressed peat moss in mines, perhaps reminding him of the mossy banks of the river Lugar where he spent his youth. Where most people would fail to notice this or perhaps admire but think no more of it, someone with a mind like William Murdoch would have been captivated by its beauty. The desire to discover how such a gem-like product could be formed from something as lowly as peat moss seems once again to have set his inventive wheels in motion. He built machinery to grind, pulverise and consolidate peat moss under great pressure into a material with 'the appearance of the finest jet' from which he made highly polished medals and jewellery. It was this ability to see how not only technology but nature could be improved upon that led to such a breathtaking range of inventions.

The mind of this remarkable man never rested, even in old age. It is said that in later years he was thinking of ways to use the force generated by people's feet and horses' hooves as they came into contact with the ground in busy city streets. With characteristic foresight he realised the possibility of harnessing wave and tidal energy in anticipation of the energy requirements of the future. In the words of Alexander Murdoch:

> '... of him in no ordinary degree it may be said that, 'having served his generation he fell asleep.'

Portrait of William Murdoch (1754-1839)

Graham Gilbert

Acknowledgements

Thanks are due to many people in particular my father James Stewart for inspiration and my husband Stanley Thomson for ideas, sound advice and constant encouragement.

The co-operation of librarians has been invaluable, especially from the University of Glasgow, Strathclyde University, the Mitchell Library, Cornish Studies Library, Birmingham City Archives and the British Library. Further help was given by curators and researchers at the Glasgow University's Hunterian Museum, the Baird Institute, Summerlee Heritage Trust, Grand Lodge Edinburgh, Wanlockhead Museum, Avery Berkel, Murdoch House and South Kensington Science Museum.

The material for this book came from many sources notably three publications: Light Without A Wick, A Man Of Little Showing and The Third Man*. This latter book, the biography of William Murdoch, explores with great depth and breadth all aspects of Murdoch's life and work. For the first time vital information is pieced together and I am indebted to author John Griffiths for kind permission to quote from his work.

My sincere thanks also to Geoff Hayes for expert advice and information, John Stewart of Clyde Computer Centre for additional historical detail as well as technical support and expertise, Stewart Burns for original artwork and Robin Gillett of brocweb.com for web design.

----

*The Third Man—The Life And Times Of William Murdoch 1754-1839, The Inventor Of Gas Lighting by John Griffiths—was published by Andre Deutsch in 1992. The hardback edition, currently out of print, is available in libraries; a future paperback edition is anticipated.

TOURIST GUIDE

SCOTLAND

Auchinleck
Kirkyard
Obelisk commemorating
famous local people including
William Murdoch
B7036 Auchinleck, Ayrshire

Biggar
Gas Works
Only remaining Scottish gas
works, now a museum.
Bust of Murdoch
*Off A702 near Cadgers Brig,
Biggar, South Lanarkshire
Daily 14.00-16.30 June-Sept.
Biggar Museum Trust*
01899 221050/221070
www.biggar-net.co.uk

Coatbridge
Summerlee Heritage Trust
Steam engines, tramway, mine,
history and exhibition area
*Off A89, off West Canal Street,
Coatbridge, Lanarkshire
Daily 10-5*
01236 431261
www.northlan.gov.uk/leisure

Culzean
Gas House, Culzean Castle
Gas works and cottage display
with replica models of
Murdoch's Steam Carriage;
Oscillating Cylinder Engine;
Sun & Planet gear. History and
photos of Murdoch.
*A719, 4 miles west of Maybole
Open daily (Apr-Oct) 10-4.
National Trust for Scotland.*
01655 884455
www.culzeancastle.net

Cumnock
Baird Institute
Near Murdoch's birthplace.
Local history, parish records,
registers, photos, model of pro-
posed Murdoch Museum
*Off A76 3 Lugar Street,
Cumnock, Ayrshire
Mon Tue Thu Fri
10.00-13.00 and 13.30-14.30*
01290 421701

Edinburgh
Royal Edinburgh Society
Later portrait of Murdoch by
Graham Gilbert
22-24 George Street, Edinburgh
<u>NB</u> Portrait in private collection

Edinburgh
Royal Museum, Edinburgh
B&W rotative beam engine
refurbished in 1999, in regular
operation on compressed air
Chambers Street, Edinburgh
Daily 10-5 (Tue 10-8 Sun 12-5)
0131 247 4219
www.nms.ac.uk

Lugar
Bellow Mill
Birthplace of William Murdoch.
Privately owned cottage, mill
ruins, riverside cave
A70 Lugar, Ayrshire
<u>NB</u> Property is privately owned

Glasgow
Mitchell Library
Local & parish records, history,
books, journals, newspapers,
archives
3 North Street, Charing Cross,
Glasgow (city centre)
0141 287 2999
www.glasgowlibraries.org

Glasgow
Museum of Transport
Drawing of Soho Foundry,
Birmingham
1 Bunhouse Road, Kelvin Hall
Glasgow. Daily 10-5 (Fri Sat 11-5)
0141 287 2628
www.glasgow.gov.uk/cls

Glasgow
People's Palace
Gas lamps
Glasgow Green, Glasgow
0141 554 0223
www.glasgowgalleries.co.uk

Greenock
James Watt Library
Library and museum with
memorabilia and letters
of James Watt
9 Union Street, Greenock
01475 715628 (library) 715624 (museum)
www.inverclyde.gov.uk

Irvine
The Big Idea
Interactive centre devoted to
inventions & inventors incl.
William Murdoch
Off A78, by bridge from Irvine
harbour, Irvine, North Ayrshire
01294 461999; 08708 404030
www.bigidea.org.uk

Kelso
Reputed site of earliest application of gas lighting in Scotland
Former coppersmith's, now shoe
shop: Bridge Street, Kelso, Borders.
www.kelso.bordernet.co.uk/
people/william-murdock

Melrose
Melrose Abbey
Founded in 1136. Burial place of the heart of Robert the Bruce. Tablet in south transept of 16th century mason, John Murdoch
Off A68 and A7
Melrose, Scottish Borders
Daily 9.30-6.30
01896 822562
www.historic-scotland.co.uk

Stirling
Hall of Heroes,
National Wallace Monument
Sixteen statues of some of Scotland's greatest men incl. William Murdoch
Off B998 1 mile NE of Stirling Castle, Abbey Craig, Stirlingshire
01786 472140
www.scottish.heartlands.org

Stirling
Smith Art Gallery and Museum
Exhibitions of art, history and archaeology. Model of Murdoch's steam carriage
Off A811, Dumbarton Road
Tue-Sat 10.30-5 Sun 2-5
01786 471917
www.smithartgallery.demon.co.uk

Wanlockhead
Mining Museum, Beam Engine
Murdoch worked here 1797. Early 19th c beam engine and lead mining museum. History incl. copies of letters between Murdoch and Watt
A797 Wanlockhead, Dumfries & Galloway
01659 74387
www.leadminingmuseum.co.uk

Historic Scotland
Longmore House, Salisbury St
Edinburgh EH9 1SH
0131 668 8800
www.historic-scotland.co.uk

VisitScotland
Scottish Tourist Information
23 Ravelston Terrace,
Edinburgh EH4 3TP
0131 332 2433
www.visitscotland.co.uk

ENGLAND

Birmingham
Avery Berkel (Soho Works site)
Murdoch's house at 13 Foundry
Lane with plaque, bust of
Murdoch, copies of documents,
museum with weights & scales
Foundry Lane, Smethwick,
West Midlands B66 2LP
Mon Tue by appointment
08709 034343 ext 1667
www.averyberkel.com

Birmingham
Central Library Archives
Archives of Soho (closed for re-
cataloguing until October 2003)
Chamberlain Square, Birmingham
0121 303 4217
www.birmingham.gov.uk

Birmingham
City Art Gallery
Painting by John Graham
Gilbert RSA of Murdoch in
early middle age
Portrait of Murdoch by
EW Papworth
Chamberlain Square, Birmingham
0121 303 2834
Picture Library 0121 303 3155
www.bmag.org.uk

Birmingham
The Parish Church of St Mary,
Handsworth
Burial place of Murdoch, Watt
& Boulton. Bust of Murdoch by
Sir Francis Chantrey in chancel
B4124 Hamstead Road, off Soho
Road, Handsworth, Birmingham

Birmingham
Museum of Science & Discovery
Model of Murdoch's steam
carriage; plaster bust;
working steam engine
B4132 Millennium Point,
Curzon Street, Birmingham
0121 202 2222
www.thinktank.ac

Birmingham
outside Register Office
Statue by W Bloye of
Boulton, Watt & Murdoch
A456 Broad Street,
Birmingham City Centre

Birmingham
Soho House
Home of Matthew Boulton
Soho Avenue, off Soho Road (A41)
Handsworth, Birmingham
0121 554 9122
www.bmag.org.uk

London
Science Museum, South
Kensington, London
Murdoch's oscillating cylinder
engine and Sun & Planet gear;
Watt lap engine and Atkinson
engine; plans for new energy
exhibition
S Kensington Underground; Bus
numbers 9, 10, 49, 52, 74, 345, C1
0870 870 4771; 0870 870 4868
www.sciencemuseum.org.uk

London
National Portrait Gallery
Two pencil drawings of
William Murdoch
by Sir Francis Chantrey
St Martin's Place, London WC2H
020 7306 0055
www.npg.org.uk

Redruth
Cornish Studies Library
History, plaster replica of
marble bust of Murdoch by Sir
Francis Chantrey
Alma Place, Redruth, Cornwall
01209 216760
cornishstudies.library@cornwall.
gov.uk

Redruth
Cornish Mines & Engines
Industrial Discovery Centre
Trevithick Road, Pool, Redruth
Cornwall
01209 315027
www.trevithicktrust.com

Redruth
Murdoch House
Murdoch's House now
Museum. Commemorative
plaque, information, history.
Annual Murdoch weekend in
June. Full-scale replica steam
carriage nearby.
Cross Street, Redruth, Cornwall
01209 215736
www.chycor.co.uk/murdoch-house

Warrington
National Gas Archives
Large bronze plaque of
Murdoch (from August 2003)
Unit 1, Europa Court, Europa
Boulevard, Warrington WA5 7TN

English Tourist Information
Thames Tower, Blacks Road,
Hammersmith, London W6 9EL
0208 846 9000
www.visitbritain.com

WHERE TO VIEW MURDOCH MEMORABILIA

Archives/Copies of Letters
Birmingham City Archives;
Murdoch House, Redruth;
Cornish Studies Library, Redruth
Wanlockhead Mining Museum

Bust/Replica Bust
by Sir Frances Chantrey
Church of St Mary, Handsworth;
The Gas House, Culzean Castle;
Birmingham Museum of Science
& Discovery; Avery Berkel, Soho;
Cornish Studies Library;
Biggar Gas Works

Bust *by DW Stephenson*
Hall of Heroes,
Wallace Monument, Stirling

Commemorative Plaques
Bellow Mill, Lugar; Murdoch
House, Redruth; Foundry Lane,
Soho (Avery Berkel); National
Gas Archives, Warrington

**Model of Proposed Murdoch
Museum**
The Baird Institute, Cumnock

**Model/Replica Model Steam
Carriage**
Redruth; Birmingham Museum
of Science & Discovery;
The Gas House, Culzean Castle;
Smith Art Gallery & Museum,
Stirling

Museums/Displays
Murdoch House, Redruth;
The Gas House, Culzean Castle;
The Baird Institute, Cumnock;
The Big Idea, Irvine

Obelisk *by John Murdoch*
Auchinleck Kirkyard, Ayrshire

Oscillating Cylinder Engine
Kensington Science Museum;
The Gas House, Culzean Castle

Portraits/Drawings
National Portrait Gallery;
Birmingham City Art Gallery

Statue *by W Bloye*
Outside Birmingham
Register Office

Sun & Planet Gear
Royal Museum of Edinburgh;
Kensington Science Museum;
The Gas House, Culzean Castle

Retorts

Inside the doors of the retort are fireclay tubes in which coal was heated to give off gas and tar. The remaining coke was later used as fuel to heat the retorts.

Condenser

Hot, tar-laden gas from the retorts passed up and down condenser pipes, cooling and losing most of the tar as liquid. In larger city gas works, this by-product was used to make aniline dyes, paints, colours, preservatives and ammonium sulphate fertiliser.

Purifier

Gas was passed into purifying tanks where a layer of powdered iron ore removed toxic hydrogen sulphide. Finally the gas was washed in tanks of water before storage.

Gas Holder

Purified gas was stored in large tanks floating in water to maintain a steady pressure in the supply.

GAS WORKS

Biggar Gas Works

Top left: Gas Holder, Showroom and Offices
Top right: Condenser and Purifiers
Bottom: Retorts

BIBLIOGRAPHY

Beam Engines *Geoffrey Hayes*
Shire Publications 2003 ISBN 0 7478 0544 X

Gifts of Athena: Historical Origins of the Knowledge Economy
Joel Mokyr Princeton University Press 2002 ISBN 0 691094837

The Lunar Men *Jenny Uglow*
Faber and Faber Limited 2002 ISBN 0 571 19647 0

Cornish Inventors *Carolyn Martin*
Tor Mark Press 2001 ISBN 0 85025 390 X

The First Freemasons: Scotland's Early Lodges & Their Members
David Stephenson Grand Lodge of Scotland 2001 ISBN 0 902324 65 9

The Last Miller *James Pearson*
Ayrshire Monographs 2000 ISBN 0 9527445 6 2

Scotland: A Traveller's History *Andrew Fisher*
Windrush Press Third Edition 1999 ISBN 1 900624 49 4

The Third Man—The Life and Times of William Murdoch
1754-1839 The Inventor of Gas Lighting *John Griffiths*
Andre Deutsch 1992 ISBN 0 233 98778 9

William Murdoch Mechanician, Maverick & Medallist
John Richard Taylor C Eng MI Gas E
Midlands Gas Association 1992

A History of Auchinleck Village and Parish *Dane Love*
1991 ISBN 0 9518128 0 7

The Man with the Timmer Hat *TD Chadwick*
The Scots Magazine February 1980

William Murdoch 'Man of Little Showing' *James A McCash*
**The College Courant—The Journal of the Glasgow University
Graduates Association** Vol Eighteen No 37 Martinmas 1966

Bibliography

William Murdoch—Faithful Servant *James A McCash*
The Chartered Mechanical Engineer July 1966

The Glasgow Herald November 1, 1964

Ayrshire at the Time of Burns Vol V *David D Murison*
Ayrshire Archaeological & Natural History Society 1959

An Obscured Scottish Genius *R Barclay Murdoch*
Gas Journal May 15, 1929

Light Without a Wick—A Centuy of Gas Lighting 1792-1892
A Sketch of William Murdoch The Inventor *Alexander Murdoch.*
Robert Maclehose Glasgow 1892

The Times September 11, 1883

The Engineer June 10, 1881

The Mechanics Magazine Vol XIX April 6-September 28, 1833

A Treatise of Mechanics, Theoretical, Practical and Descriptive
Olinthus Gregory Volume II George Kearsley London 1806

LIST OF QUOTATIONS

LIST OF ILLUSTRATIONS

Photographs & Illustrations

Original Illustrations
by Stewart Burns, D.A.

AVAILABLE FROM BOOKSHOPS, INTERNET AND BY MAIL ORDER

THE SCOT WHO LIT THE WORLD
THE STORY OF WILLIAM MURDOCH, INVENTOR OF GAS LIGHTING
by Janet Thomson   ISBN 0 9530013 2 6   Price £6.99
To order on the internet:
www.williammurdoch.com

*

For mail order, please send cheque to:
Janet Thomson
5 Circus Place
Dennistoun
Glasgow G31 2JJ
Scotland, UK

UK customers please add £1.00 P&P for each book
(£2.50 per book outwith the UK)

Other Books by Janet Thomson

COMMON GARDEN ENEMIES
A GARDENING GUIDE STARRING
SLUGS, DEER, SQUIRRELS, MOLES, MICE, CATS, BIRDS, FOXES, SHEEP & RABBITS
ISBN 0 9530013 1 8   Price £4.99

*

GARDENING WITH THE ENEMY
A GUIDE TO RABBIT-PROOF GARDENING
ISBN 0 9530013 0 X   Price £3.99

www.rabbitgarden.com

INDEX

First published in Scotland in 2003 by

JANET THOMSON
5 Circus Place
Glasgow G31 2JJ
Scotland
www.williammurdoch.com

First edition June 2003

ISBN 0-9530013-2-6

9 780953 001323 >

Computer equipment supplied by
Clyde Computer Centre, Unit A4, Fullarton Road, Glasgow G32 8YL
www.glasgowcomputing.com

Printed in Glasgow